AN INTRODUCTION TO

DRAWING
ANIMALS

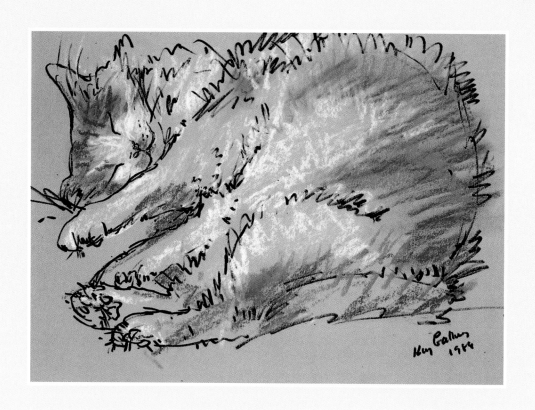

AN INTRODUCTION TO

DRAWING
ANIMALS

anatomy ● movement ● perspective ● character ● composition

Kay Gallwey

NEW
BURLINGTON
BOOKS

A QUINTET BOOK

Published in 2004 by New Burlington Books
6 Blundell Street
London N7 9BH

Reprinted 2004

ISBN 1 86155 431 1

This book was designed and produced by
Quintet Publishing Limited
6 Blundell Street
London N7 9BH

Editors: Robert Stewart, Shaun Barrington
Art Director: Peter Bridgewater
Designer: Linda Moore
Illustrator: Stefan Oliver

Creative Director: Richard Dewing
Publisher: Oliver Salzmann

Typeset in Great Britain by
Central Southern Typesetters, Eastbourne
Manufactured by Regent Publishing Services, Ltd.
Printed in Singapore by Star Standard Industries Pte Ltd.

Picture Credits

K.F. Barker from Rogues' Gallery, (pub. William Heinemann Ltd.):
p37 (b), p39 (t), p63 (t, b); Richard Bell: p79, p82; Stephen Crowther:
p39 (b), p124, p125; C.M. Dixon: p10, p11 (t, b), p44, p52; London
Transport Museum: p108; Michael Kitchen-Hurle: p37 (t), p40 (t);
The National Gallery: p64; Private Collection, (picture courtesy of the Courtauld
Institute of Art): p60; Victoria and Albert Museum: p38 (t), p40 (b).

While every effort has been made on the part of the Publisher
to acknowledge all sources and copyright holders, Quintet Publishing
would liketo apologize if any omissions have been made.

CONTENTS

INTRODUCTION

In the late 1960's drawing, to put it mildly, became very devalued and plaster casts that students had been drawing for decades were ritualistically smashed. Life drawing was deeply frowned upon and the graphics technique and style in art became all. The baby was thrown out with the bathwater and the airbrush and Grant projector took over.

Luckily for me I was taught to draw whether I wanted to or not (and sometimes I really did not want to) by some extraordinary teachers.

In 1954 at the City and Guilds School of Art in London I was taught drawing by Middleton Todd RA, Robin Gutherie RA, and Henry Wilkinson, and sculpture by Mr Bissett. I went on from there to the Royal Academy, where Mr. Fleetwood Walker, Professor Albert Richardson, and Peter Greenham drummed into their students' heads how important drawing really was. We did six weeks of life drawing to prove we could draw before even being allowed anywhere near the painting and sculpture school. The older I get, the more thankful I am that I was taught by these great drawers.

Artists who have made the leap from realism to other forms of expression, if they are worth their salt at all, have always been grounded in drawing. Or if not, a lot of them have decided to go back to it. From prehistoric cavemen, to Egyptian muralists, to Leonardo, to Picasso, to De Kooning, and many more that I could mention, there have been artists who could draw like a dream and from this springboard took off in any direction they desired.

So far I have been writing about professional artists, people who earn their living and provide other people's in the world of art markets and galleries, with all their changes in tastes and fashion. What you and I are concerned with, however, is getting something down on paper that represents the animal in front of us and in the process expressing ourselves and having fun doing so.

This book will try to show you ways in which you can put something on paper that will give satisfaction, and even joy. First and foremost a knowledge of anatomy is extremely important—it provides the framework on which we hang all our drawing. Understanding the principles of perspective, proportion, texture, and character all have their place. We shall also look at what professional artists have done in the past and, I hope, learn from them.

Why do you want to draw animals instead of (or perhaps as well as) landscapes or portraits? In my case it is because I love to draw things that move, and animals, like dancers, move beautifully and make beautiful shapes. Horses galloping, dogs alert, cats stretching, kittens playing or just lying down and sleeping, are some of the domestic subjects available.

BELOW **Study for a painting. Charcoal and Conté on colored paper.**

Many of us have animals we love and we want to capture the individual and beloved characteristics of our particular pet. Or we may have an affinity for wild animals, the strong slow-moving elephant, the gentle giraffe whose beautiful eyes have the longest eyelashes ever, the furry giant panda, or the spotted ocelot. All of us who want to draw animals love them and this should be at the center of our drawing.

Look at the pages of animal portraits on pages 36–40, and consider how each one, in its way, is a success. Your knowledge of your own pet, its character, its funny ways, its dislikes and likes, gives you the advantage that you can put these down on paper truly. Do not ever be put off by not getting the legs quite right, for instance, though I trust this book will help with this aspect; while the importance of the rightness of the legs cannot be denied, if the

portrait has *that* look, communicates *that* character, of *that* certain animal, then you have succeeded.

From the earliest prehistoric cave paintings people have drawn what is closest and most important to them. Have you noticed how little children can draw with fun and sometimes surprising accuracy? My own daughter drew her father when she was four. It was a big oval, some wispy hair, and a soft wiggle for a mouth, but boy was it just like her dad. With no training in how to draw but with the intimate knowledge of how he looked that was inside her head, she had, without any doubt, got it in one.

Try and maintain this childlike way of looking at things. Try for the line, that thing that makes the subject who and what it is. Do not get put off the scent. Then, with the knowledge and the different techniques I shall give you, and with the final and most important

ingredient of all, your own talent and judgment—and we *all* have some, just forget that teacher at school who said you couldn't draw —and do what and how you feel; most important of all, how and what you *see*. After all, it is your picture, isn't it?

In this book, because it is about how to draw animals in the most practical sense, we need not go into art history too much. You can find that out in an art history book and it will almost invariably deal with drawing and painting together. It is interesting, however, to know something of the beginnings of the materials we have to draw with: charcoal, pencils, and early pigments for color.

BELOW **Right from the curly tail to the muzzle, and from the fat, round, rough-skinned body to the tiny feet, this pig has been caught on paper by someone of only three and a half.**

1
MATERIALS AND EQUIPMENT

The earliest known sources of pigment are found in the paintings of prehistoric cavemen 25,000B.C. French Cave paintings dated between 10,000 and 15,000B.C. show that burnt wood and bones, chalks, and various earths produced yellow and brown.

In Egypt 2000–1000B.C., cinnabar, realgar, azurite, orpiment, and malachite were used to produce red, orange, blue, yellow, and green. The Romans extracted Tyrian purple from the humble whelk and obtained a green called verdigris by corroding copper plate. In A.D.1200 Arabs discovered ultramarine by extracting blue particles from lapis lazuli.

DRAWING MATERIALS

The first graphite pencil was made in 1662. Gums, resin, and glue were added to extend the graphite, which allowed it to be pressed into wood. Another way of supporting the graphite was to use a holder called a porte-crayon.

Faber started a pencil company in 1761. Napoleon asked him to develop a substitute formulation because he was worried about importation of scarce materials. Faber had been using three parts graphite to one part sulfur; now he came up with a mixture of clay, graphite, water, and paste that hardened when baked in kilns and was then pressed into grooves cut in wood. This eventually led to the production of colored pencils, which are made from kaolin, wax, and dyes.

Charcoal is basically burnt wood (as used by the early cavemen). Artists' charcoal has to be burnt and processed in a special way to keep air out and so produce a consistent intensity of blackness.

It seems that drawing has been natural to us from as far back as any relics we have unearthed can tell us. Whether the cave paintings were produced for pure decoration or used in ritual, we do not know. Children do it naturally; it is a form of communication and a form of inner satisfaction and journeying. Bon voyage! There was a time when artists used burnt sticks to draw with. Later artists had their raw pigments mixed by their apprentices. Nowadays it is easy to go to the art stores and buy from a vast range of products, though you can still buy the raw pigment and mix your own colors with suitable media if you wish. Preference on materials is a matter for the individual and only by trial and error and lots of practice will you find out for yourself what medium you best like to draw animals. As each technique is considered we will discover in detail each stage of preparation and use to help you select appropriate materials for the occasion.

If you are going to draw from life you will find, of course, that animals, unlike trees, flowers, landscapes, and nudes, are not going to stand around and wait for you to draw them. So, if you are running around the house trying to draw your kitten, or in a field with a grazing horse, it is sensible not to encumber yourself with bottles of ink and nib-tipped pens. Again, there is nothing worse, as I know, than taking an inadequately packed drawing satchel and finding yourself miles out in a field, or at the zoo, and discovering you have left your

LEFT **This jug from Melos bears witness to the fact that paintings of animals were used as far back as the 2nd Millenium B.C. as decoration.**

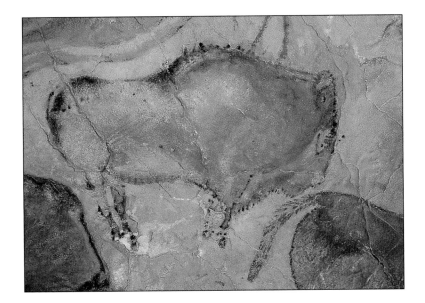

LEFT Paleolithic cave painting from the Altimara caves in Spain.

BELOW Paleolithic cave painting of an aurochs and horses, found in Lascaux, France.

favorite pencil or technical pen behind and have brought the wrong sketchbook for doing washes.

Should you be at home in the studio, not sketching a live animal, but working from photographs and sketching and drawing in detail, then you can go to delicate media such as fine pens for cross-hatching, complicated washes, and difficult techniques.

In general, book illustrators of animals tend to use inks, or ink and wash or watercolor rather than pastels or charcoal because they are easier to send to printers and less messy for everybody to deal with. Unless thoroughly fixed, which tends to detract from the light and color of the medium, pastels will smudge and drop when moved. They do not travel well and for this reason are more expensive to reproduce.

Line and wash is excellent for sketching moving animals. There are lots of ways of using line and wash. One is pen and wash, the other is a fine paintbrush used as a pen for the line and a broader brush for the wash. You can use either inks or watercolor. Then there is a range of mixed media we shall discuss later.

Instead of buying a full range of expensive materials I recommend a beginner's package, which enables you to to sample techniques without too much expense. Then when you find the one or two techniques that satisfy your need you can add to your beginner's package slowly, gradually building up a comprehensive range of materials according to need and experience. A lot of expensive equipment does not turn you into a good animal drawer.

PAPER

As with the beginner's pack of media you should start with a few inexpensive things. There is nothing more frightening and confidence sapping than being given an expensive drawing book. You feel that every mark should be special and it can make you very downhearted when things do not turn out so well. This is especially true when drawing animals where, unlike flowers or other elements in a still life for instance, you have no control over the subject. It is best to buy a fair amount of sugar paper in neutral colors and a good, reasonably priced, 20 x 10in. spiral bound sketchbook.

As you progress in confidence and ability, there is no end to the possibilities of texture, color, weight, and price of your paper. There are extremes of surfaces as smooth as marble watercolor paper to extremely rough and tinted pastel paper, in an infinite variety of color and quality of paper. Drawing paper also comes in huge rolls for those who wish to draw big, although this is not usually recommended for the beginner and a roll can drive you mad fighting to make it flat and cutting it to the right size.

Drawing pads, if they are thick enough, can be used without a drawing board, especially those with spiral binding as you can tuck a drawing under when you have finished it without spoiling it and you can tear them out individually without wrecking the pad. There are many types and sizes of these pads with different weights of paper, and smoothness and roughness of texture. It is better, as a beginner, to start with smooth paper (cold pressed or NOT).

Less useful is the hard-backed sketchbook without spiral binding, which is also available in different weights of paper and smoothness. While easy to carry around, unlike the spiral bound sketchbook it is not easy to extricate completed sketches from the book.

BELOW **Paper is available in all sizes, weights, and textures, and to suit every type of medium.**

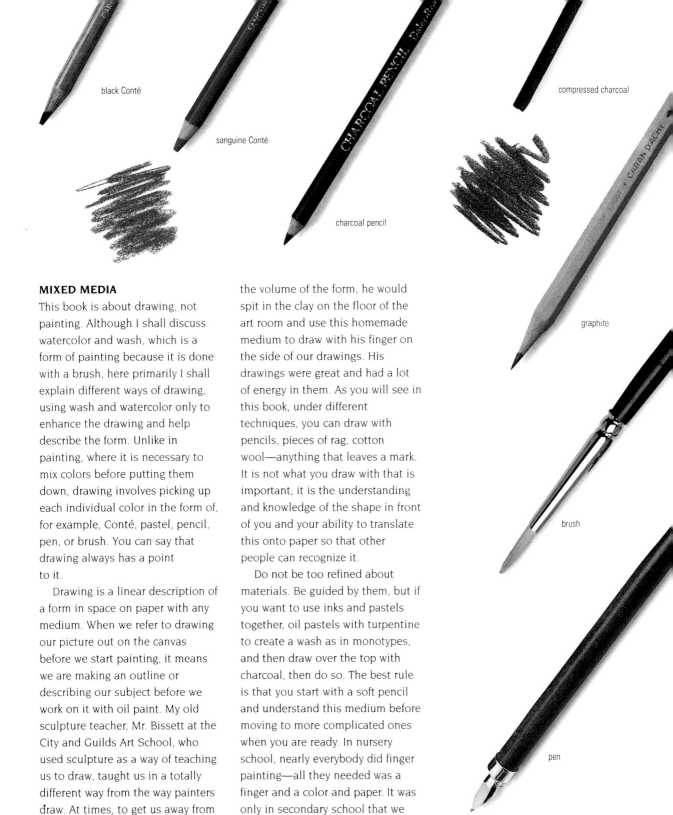

black Conté

sanguine Conté

compressed charcoal

charcoal pencil

graphite

brush

pen

MIXED MEDIA

This book is about drawing, not painting. Although I shall discuss watercolor and wash, which is a form of painting because it is done with a brush, here primarily I shall explain different ways of drawing, using wash and watercolor only to enhance the drawing and help describe the form. Unlike in painting, where it is necessary to mix colors before putting them down, drawing involves picking up each individual color in the form of, for example, Conté, pastel, pencil, pen, or brush. You can say that drawing always has a point to it.

Drawing is a linear description of a form in space on paper with any medium. When we refer to drawing our picture out on the canvas before we start painting, it means we are making an outline or describing our subject before we work on it with oil paint. My old sculpture teacher, Mr. Bissett at the City and Guilds Art School, who used sculpture as a way of teaching us to draw, taught us in a totally different way from the way painters draw. At times, to get us away from the finicky business of fine drawing on white paper and in his determination to *make* us describe

the volume of the form, he would spit in the clay on the floor of the art room and use this homemade medium to draw with his finger on the side of our drawings. His drawings were great and had a lot of energy in them. As you will see in this book, under different techniques, you can draw with pencils, pieces of rag, cotton wool—anything that leaves a mark. It is not what you draw with that is important; it is the understanding and knowledge of the shape in front of you and your ability to translate this onto paper so that other people can recognize it.

Do not be too refined about materials. Be guided by them, but if you want to use inks and pastels together, oil pastels with turpentine to create a wash as in monotypes, and then draw over the top with charcoal, then do so. The best rule is that you start with a soft pencil and understand this medium before moving to more complicated ones when you are ready. In nursery school, nearly everybody did finger painting—all they needed was a finger and a color and paper. It was only in secondary school that we became frightened out of our natural abilities, probably by people who could not draw anyway.

DRAWING BOARDS

A good drawing board is essential; one you can rely on, that will hold thumbtacks to fix the paper. Avoid anything like a thin plywood. Treat yourself to a proper board from a shop instead of improvizing. You can work with a board on an easel, but lots of people do not. They use drawing boards against a table or chair. If you have space in your house an easel is useful for indoor work because you can stand back from it and see the effect you are creating. This is just as important for drawers as for painters; it is the steadying role of the drawing board that is essential. There are small folding easels for outdoors, which are even more useful if they have carrying pouches on them.

In the house you will find your animal for sketching in all sorts of places—in patches of sunlight, under furniture, on the sofa, or curled up in a linen cupboard— where you cannot lay things out according to plan. I have found myself resting on the banisters, constructing a makeshift easel by leaning the drawing board against an upright chair or just sitting with it on my legs and knees. This is why you need a smaller drawing board as well as a large one.

Use thumbtacks, or masking tape to hold the paper in place on your drawing board. A clipboard is acceptable as well. Drawing blocks are especially useful for drawing or painting outside; they come in any weight of paper but are more expensive than single sheeted paper. Another problem is that the paper under the one you are drawing on can easily become dented or even wet if you use too much wash. Take great care in taking off a finished sheet since it can rip and ruin your picture. Using these blocks will eliminate using a drawing board but it is wise to have an artists' folder with you in which to store sheets of finished work.

WORKPLACE

The ideal workplace is a room with plenty of space and light, and a north light if possible because it is constant.

You need a clean, large table and a smaller one you can move around with you. Smallish boxes are handy. You may obtain some old cigar boxes from a tobacco store for the purpose or any old box will do to keep your things in. Label them so that you can reach them quickly, and also keep them out of the way of children and animals. You cannot blame children if they see your lovely colors and want to have a go. You need at least a couple of artists' folders with tie tops, and a flat surface like a plan chest to keep your paper and finished drawings flat in a drawer or on a large shelf.

Ink wash or watercolor work can be put in plastic folders or envelopes to keep it clean. Never put chalk or pastel drawings in or under plastic—it pulls the surface artwork off and destroys the picture.

ABOVE **You must always tape your paper to your surface before working on it. This will prevent buckling if you are using watercolor, but also reduce tearing and creasing when using other media.**

If possible, have shelves or closets where you can leave your materials so that they can be easily accessed; this also enables you to see when you are running out of something.

It is important to keep a space on the wall where you can pin up your latest work to enable you to sit in front of it or walk past it daily. Keep looking at it. You will see these works differently as the light changes and you will realize how you need to alter them, and appreciate bits you feel you have captured well. This space for displaying your work should be kept private if at all possible as other people's comments may cloud your judgement.

It is important to be able to make a mess. Equally, after each picture is finished, not just a sketch, but the full picture, you should make a point of clearing away your references and filing them, clean your mixing palettes, and wash jugs. Put everything back in its proper place. Make sure brushes and all utensils are clean and well looked after before you start on your next project. These steps should become a routine for you as you go along.

If not drawing at an easel, lean your drawing board against a table edge, but make sure you have a chair that supports your back well. You may have enormous enthusiasm for the picture, with all the references and materials laid

out properly, but it will be quite useless and unproductive if you end up getting a roaring pain between your shoulder blades after half an hour.

If possible, you need enough room to put your picture either on an easel or up against a wall to allow you continually to stand back and appraise it. Many artists know the feeling of excitedly working on detail for a couple of hours only to stand back and wonder where the life of the picture has gone.

All fixing should be done by or preferably outside a window. Fixative can certainly make you feel a bit heady and may injure your lungs over time if you are not careful. You will need to save glass jars, and any large plastic containers with their tops cut off and washed out thoroughly—they

are wonderful for use in the studio. There are lots of expensive brush holders and paint pots available through art stores, but nothing beats a glass jar.

It is also a good idea to have a plastic bag full of rags. Not just any old rags—T-shirts, old sheets, shirts, blouses, and other natural-fiber clothes are ideal as rags. Anything nylon or hard is useless. When you have some spare time, sit and cut up these discarded items into rectangular pieces roughly 12 x 10in. They will be invaluable for wiping watercolors and monotype plates, and for wiping

out jars and palettes, and cleaning brushes. It is advisable to have a liquid soap handy and also paint cleaner for your own hands and for oil painting brushes or those used for monotypes.

As this book only covers using paint as a drawing medium, I shall not go into media, but you will need two types of turpentine—one good quality distilled turpentine for use with oil pastels and an ordinary white spirit for cleaning up after yourself. Lastly, you will need access to plenty of clean water as the secret of all wash and watercolor is the continuous renewal of clean water in your jars. You should always have two glass jars handy—one for washing the brushes and one for the ink or watercolor wash.

DRAWING

The simple but important rule of how to draw with anything—whether pencil, inks, watercolors, or any other medium—is first look, then think, then draw. Thinking, looking, and understanding are extremely important, for without these abilities you cannot develop your artistic talent.

It is no use having the radio on, talking to people, and trying to cook a dinner at the same time. Above all, you must try to develop the ability to concentrate. You simply cannot visualize something in your brain and try to describe it on paper while worrying about something else. If you watch a child drawing even in the most crowded room with a chalk and a piece of paper on the floor, you will see someone totally focused on what they are doing, brows knitted, tongue between the teeth and eyes on the page. Nothing interferes between the brain and the hand. Complete absorption is the key and you must practice very hard to obtain it. Like meditation, you only realize you have achieved it after the event.

In the same way that in meditation or T'ai Chi you start with small exercises in the hope of achieving the whole, the drawer must also start with simple things. The imagination is something to be cultivated and respected. You cannot be a Redon or a Chagall without immense training in excluding the outside world and concentrating on your inner world. There are two forms of exercises—the imaginative and the real. The real is easier; just look at something like a ball or a box and then, without looking again, draw it from memory. Your sketchbook should not be only for subjects drawn from life. When you are watching something like a concert, or you are at a party, try and remember as many details as you can as well as the overall impression. Use whatever medium comes to hand when you get home, to draw what you have seen.

People can teach you and can criticize your work when drawing the external world, but if you have the technical ability to put things on paper, then it is up to you and your imagination what you produce after that. It is a matter of *De gustibus non est disputandum*, which means "there can be no argument about matters of taste." You may like Picasso and not like Chagall, but no one can deny that either is a great artist.

Jean Clair's book on Henri Cartier-Bresson beautifully describes the task of drawing; "The perpetual movement of the eye back and forth from the model

stops the hand from indulging in fantasies and the eye from being overwhelmed by the model's beauty. This movement, this weighing up of many factors is the essence of drawing." (Jean Clair. *Line by Line – The Drawings of Cartier-Bresson*. Thames and Hudson Ltd., 1989.)

Looking at the work of an artist like Cartier-Bresson gives us excitement and encouragement to go on. In the end, the only way to learn to draw animals is to learn to draw everything else as well. Constant looking, constant thinking, and constant drawing is the key. Have a small sketchbook with you at all times and draw something, even if it is a matchbox, every day. The eye and the hand need never-ending practice.

If you commit yourself to one drawing class a week or draw just when you feel like it, it will take you a long time to learn to draw well; as with any exercise, you may not feel you are getting anywhere. However, it is the practice that will get you there in the end. You will be surprised to see the progress you make. Diligence has its own rewards. Keep your sketchbook to yourself so you are not constantly admired or criticized. This is not finished work; this is learning.

OPPOSITE, LEFT, AND ABOVE Only with a lot of practice can you learn to draw with any great accuracy. It is important to keep looking and drawing until you get it right. The more you practice the more you will notice. Look at these three drawings, for example. In each one a cat is sleeping. Note, however, that the position is different every time, primarily for maximum comfort. Only by constant looking and drawing will you even notice this, let alone be able to draw it.

It is sometimes falsely imagined that willpower and talent are all that the artist needs, and because art is always looked at immediately in class or at home, expectations run high. No one would expect you to be able jump a horse over a fence straight away, tap dance, or do any other thing right from the start, but people expect some sort of likeness if you are doing a portrait and tend to judge you on it. Have patience with yourself and do not be downhearted when things do not come out the way you wanted. The main point is that if you draw more and more, you *will* get better and better. Just as a surgeon has to be a general doctor first, so the artist has to learn to draw a vast range of things before finally becoming an animal artist.

Try to draw as many moving things as possible, for instance someone cooking or dancing or just talking to another person, with their weight on a particular leg as they go. Or ask someone in your house to walk across a room, pausing every two to three minutes. This will make you go for the important things first, as you have to with animals. Draw anything you have on the table—salt and pepper, a pot, or a bowl of fruit. This will teach you composition and detail. Just fill book after book with sketches and you will be surprised how much better you get. Try drawing while on a bus or train, relying on the quickness of your eye and your memory for detail. Just very swift sketches of the things that catch your eye are a very good exercise.

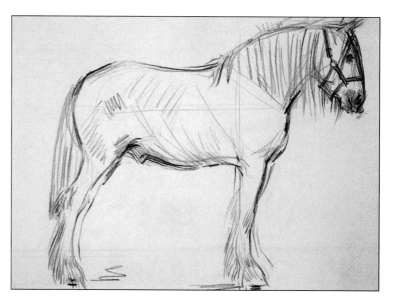

RIGHT, TOP TO BOTTOM With ample practice you should soon be producing sketches accurate enough to draw from.

2
ANATOMY

Without a knowledge of anatomy it is impossible to get weight and proportions right. In sculpture you begin with an armature. The act of building an armature guides the sculptor as to the final shape. In drawing you do not actually have to draw the skeleton first, but it helps to be able to see it in the form that you draw. The shape the animal makes is seen best by first imagining how the skeleton stands in relation to the posture an animal takes up.

UNDERSTANDING ANATOMY

In some ways four-legged animals are a little like a hammock with four supports—a body (hammock) suspended between four points (legs). This difference between human beings and animals determines the difference in how body weight is distributed and carried. The skeleton is evolved by the animal's lifestyle and its environment and enables it to deal with its particular world. For instance, giraffes have a long neck to reach leaves; monkeys have long arms to swing from trees; cheetahs are built for speed.

ABOVE Armed with a good knowledge of anatomy you should have the confidence and ability to sketch accurately from life.

On top of this skeleton is the muscle formation and fat. Look at the difference between a fast-moving greyhound and a sedentary panda. A study of anatomy helps in discerning the differences and the similarities between animals and, therefore, their different characteristics and shape.

Let us look at the skeleton, then proportion, muscle and fat and, finally, hair and fur—aspects that animals have in common with one another—and then some of the differences between animals. We shall further explore the implications of these factors for drawing.

A study of these points should assist in determining the basic line and shapes and proportions in your drawings. Examples covered in this section deal mainly with dogs, cats, and horses, but I have also included some wild animals.

The more thorough the understanding of anatomy, the greater is the appreciation of shapes that animals make when they are still and the easier it is to understand the shapes they make in motion. Much of the fear of drawing animals is due to the lack of such knowledge. A knowledge of anatomy in your head gives you the courage to go ahead and draw things you never thought you could, because you understand the shape you see. If a fox crosses the road in front of your car and you can immediately recognize the bones

ABOVE Sketching from life is rewarding, and maintains the life and character of the subject, which is often lost when drawing from photography.

under the skin, then as soon as you get the chance you can sketch this animal although you have only seen it for a second.

Therefore, instead of working from photographs all the time, armed with a knowledge of anatomy you can start drawing from life. It enables you to move from a reliance on photography to filling a

sketchbook with examples of the many types of animals you may see, such as the fox on the road, raccoons, rabbits, or zoo animals; later you can make a final picture based on these drawings and sketches if you so wish.

Without a knowledge of anatomy, of the way the fox moved and where it put its weight and how its bone structure moved under the fur, when you want to draw or recreate it on paper, it becomes a meaningless lump of fur.

All drawing is description of form in space. Its foundation is anatomy.

SKELETONS

All skeletons have in common a skull, a spine, and either arms and legs or fore and hind legs. A rib cage protects lungs and inner organs, heart and kidneys, and the pelvis protects the reproductive organs. This is the frame on which the body is carried. On top of this is muscle and fat formation and on top of that hair or fur, which again alters the animal's shape. You will notice the change of shape with animals that have more hair. For example, you will find a collie dog often has the shape of a greyhound underneath its thick fur and hair. So you will need to see something akin to a greyhound skeleton although you are drawing a collie.

The main difference between animals and human beings is that we stand upright and have arms instead of forelegs. We put all our weight on our legs and feet, freeing our arms to do other things. Monkeys and some other animals have this in common with us.

The other animals are four-legged and there are differences among them. Nongrazing animals like cats and dogs have paws, while mostly those that graze, carry, or pull, have hooves, either whole like horses, or cleft like goats and pigs.

All the animals we are considering have skulls, spines, legs, and paws, hooves or hands but have very different length and density of the bones. Generally, the lighter the animal the faster it goes. An animal like a cheetah has a very light frame, small skull, high chest, long forelegs, and immensely powerful hind legs and it is very long in the thigh. Its frame enables it to reach the speeds it can.

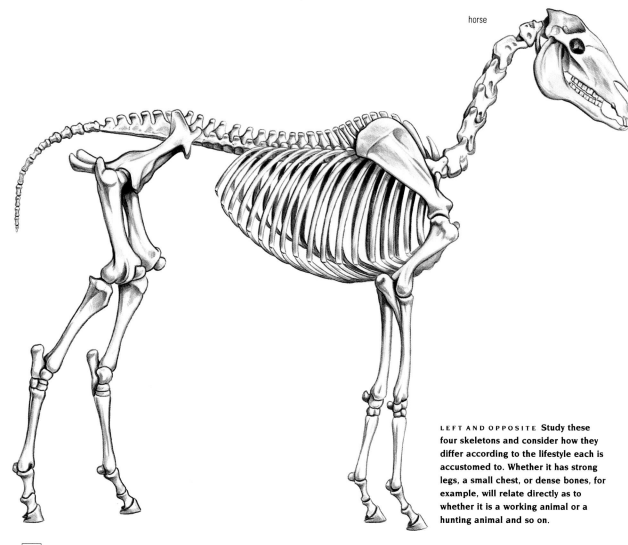

horse

LEFT AND OPPOSITE **Study these four skeletons and consider how they differ according to the lifestyle each is accustomed to. Whether it has strong legs, a small chest, or dense bones, for example, will relate directly as to whether it is a working animal or a hunting animal and so on.**

The bulldog, who has a huge breadth of chest, a heavy skull, wide mouth, big ribs, small rump, usually fat short front legs and the heaviness of bone which prevents any form of real speed in movement, has huge power and weight to fight. These animals were originally bred to fight bulls.

L E F T The nature of the cheetah's anatomy allows it to reach speeds of up to 60 miles per hour.

B E L O W Compare this elephant with the cheetah (above). Its build is much larger and sturdier, with relatively short legs and bulky body.

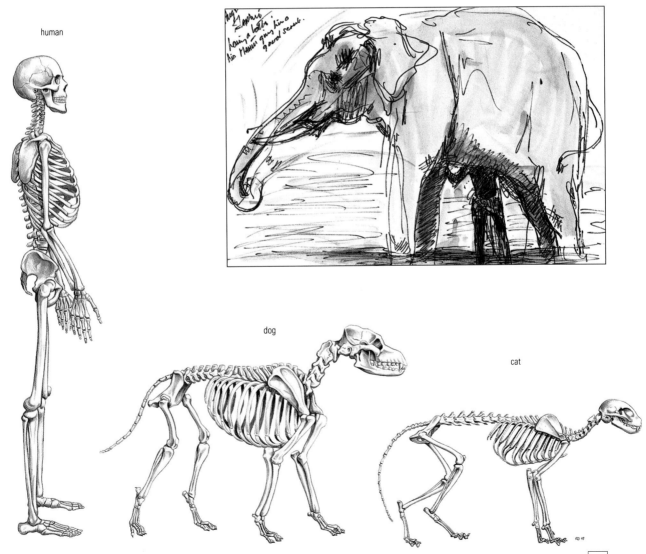

human

dog

cat

The racehorse, of course, is a very different build from the cart-horse. The racehorse has light bones and an altogether thinner build, lighter muscles, fine hair and very sensitive skin. He is built for speed. The cart-horse, on the other hand, has heavy bones, usually shorter legs, a very powerful chest and rump, is more muscular around the withers and neck, has a heavier head and rougher hair. He is built for heavy work.

Horses have hooves that are hard, shiny and slippery, but very tough; unlike cats, which have claws as well as paws and are very light and have an extremely supple bone structure. The longest muscle on a cat is along its spine. Cats can shin up trees and go over fences with remarkable agility, as we know.

Dogs also have paws but, unlike cats, they do not have sharp claws and so they cannot climb trees or cling to things. However, because of their size and the lightness of their skeleton, they tend to be agile and lithe in movement, unlike a cart-horse or an elephant, and because of the size, structure and strength of their teeth and jaw, they are very good fighters and hunters.

LEFT **Cart-horse**

LEFT **Racehorse**

THE OVERALL LINE

The most important point about drawing a subject that moves quickly and is constantly changing its position, once you have an understanding of its skeleton in your head, is to forget all detail. Do not be waylaid by the fur, hair, or eyes, just see and draw *the line* the animal makes from tip to toes, describe its shape and what it is actually doing at that moment.

This overall line should encompass and carry the eye over the whole form; more about this in the Sketchbooks section on pages 112–117 where the quicker you draw the more you need to adhere to this rule. One line can describe the character, shape and movement of an animal. Even if you are working from photographs, you must look for this line. Always aim for the essence that makes this animal and this pose different from any other. The line depends on understanding the distribution of weight and where this weight is put when a movement is made. The line that you see must be recognizable immediately, telling you what is happening and the shape that is being made; for instance if you look at a sketch of a Spanish dancer, male or female, you know by the *line* of the drawing what they are and the type of dancing they are doing.

In a standing human being this line flows from the top of the head, and runs down the spine to the weight taken on either leg, depending on the activity of the subject. As animals have four legs and may lie down a great deal, the line will take in the curve of the head, the line of the spine, and the tail if it has one. If it is lying down or stretching, as a cat does, the line will take in the length of its four

ABOVE **The line of movement is recognizable at a single glance, and is essential in gaining an insight into character, shape and weight distribution.**

legs and the curve of its body. Just as the Spanish dancer holds the castanets high and arches her back, so a cat will stretch its front legs, a

horse will arch its neck, a monkey will hang by one arm and a meercat will stay still for hours on its back legs.

This integral descriptive line is the point of drawing. It immediately defines what the artist is trying to communicate on paper. For you or anyone who sees it, it is an immediate language.

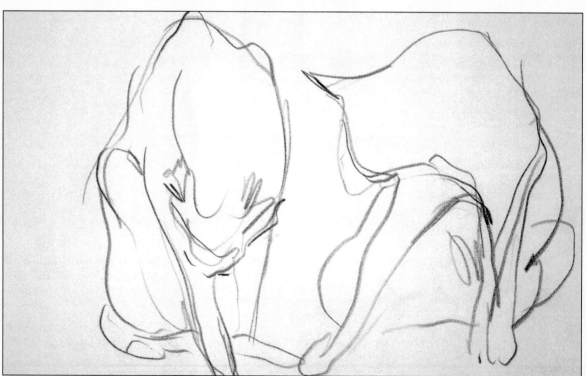

ABOVE AND OPPOSITE Study these cats and consider how the line of movement changes in each case, and how it defines the

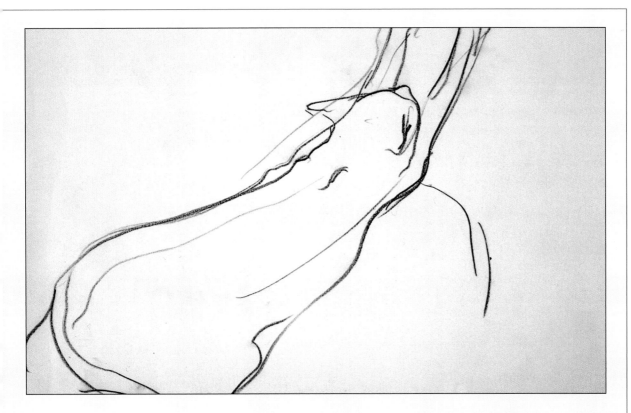

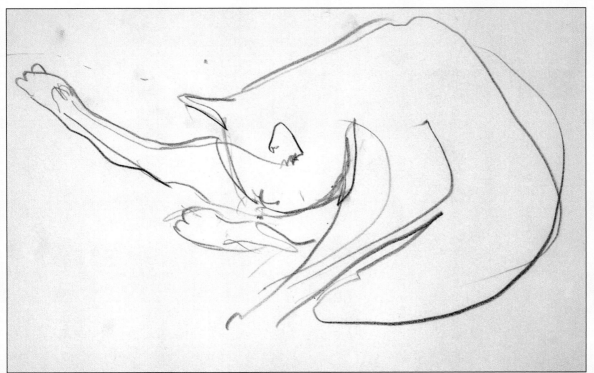

movements of the cat as it sleeps, stretches, and washes.

PROPORTIONS

Joints, as part of the skeleton, have to be noted and understood, because where joints are, limbs bend. And where bending limbs are, there is movement.

Knowing the skeleton also helps with the proportions of the animal. Note the contrast, for instance, between the extreme shortness of shoulder blade and enormous length of forearm to the ankle on an Italian greyhound, and the enormous breadth and heaviness of chest but shortness of leg on a bulldog. If you can get these proportions right then the character of that dog and its breed comes through in the drawing.

ABOVE Bulldog, charcoal, Conté, chalk

LEFT Italian greyhound, soft pencil

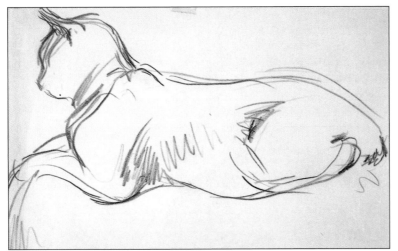

Proportions, of course, also vary in each particular breed of animal; for instance, some cats are fat and some are thin.

Also animals change with age. Take cats as an example. One way in which you can tell a kitten from a grown cat is because newly born kittens have heads that are much larger, when compared to their bodies, and their ears and tail are tiny. An older kitten grows larger ears and eyes. Compare this with a full-grown cat, which will have a larger, more powerful body. The head will have refined, the ears will be in proportion and the tail and legs longer, and, as old age sets in, it will shrink and change the way it moves, becoming more diffident.

ABOVE **Older cat, pencil**

LEFT **Here is a month-old puppy and a three-month-old puppy. The month-old puppy has a large head compared to the rest of its body, its eyes are small and closed, its feet tiny and unformed, the coat smooth, and you can see that the only thing on its mind is its mother, feeding, warmth, and sleep.**

Two months later the puppy's body is large and full, the feet fat and fluffy, the eyes are bigger and open, and the coat much thicker and rougher. The puppy's mind has broadened considerably. He still loves his mom, food, and sleep, but is inquisitive, playful, full of energy, and able to give love and attention to his brothers and sisters and anyone else who will play with him. He is beginning to assume his own character.

This is also true of the larger animals such as elephants where you can see clearly the different proportions. A baby elephant with its charming little wriggly trunk, little ears, and hairy body, contrasts with its mother's long powerful trunk, big ears, and huge hairless body. As well as calling on your knowledge of anatomy for the actual proportions of an animal you also need to do so when drawing it in perspective. A horse viewed from behind, for instance, must be drawn in perspective and in the proportions you know that a horse must have.

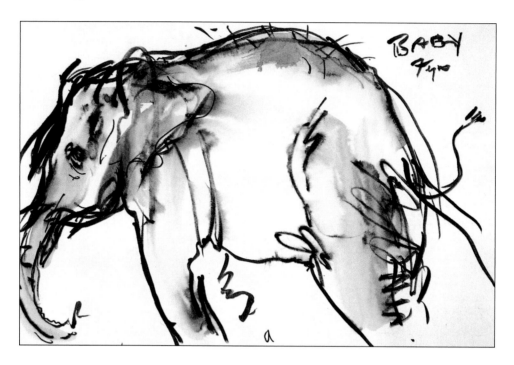

MUSCLE, HAIR, AND FUR

Having, at last, the line and proportion of the skeleton in your head, the animal must be fleshed out with muscle. A cart horse and a racehorse may be the same height, although cart horses are usually bigger, but because of their difference in function and breeding they will have a different proportion of muscle and consequently achieve a different movement.

With animals such as horses, short-haired dogs, and cats, you will be able to see the muscle forms and also how the muscles lengthen or contract when the animal moves. It will be more difficult drawing a Pyrenean mountain dog or Persian cat, and you will be forced to rely on what you have learned about the

ABOVE AND RIGHT Despite the rough, heavy coat of this deerhound, it is still possible to detect the shape of its skull, spine, limbs, and muscles. The overall shape is not dissimilar to that of a greyhound, and yet the mass of fur makes it look very different.

skeleton beneath the fur. The best way of understanding the shape an animal makes, especially if it is furry, is to feel it. When you put a heavy-coated golden collie in the bath and wash it, you will see it is as thin and fragile and as delicately shaped as a greyhound; it is the same shape but a little heavier. It is not necessary to actually give the dog a bath, just shut your eyes and feel the shape it is.

Hair, fur, coloring, and markings are what define not only the species but the character of an animal. We know a leopard by its spots and we recognize the cat next door, and its character, by details such as its black moustache and one black eye. Markings and coloring can create character. It is because of this that the length and luxuriance of a Persian cat's fur give it the character of a spoiled princess, while the rough, scruffy hair of a terrier gives it the jaunty character of a street urchin.

Hair and fur are wonderful to draw and paint. Once you have achieved the anatomy of the animal and the line, it is important to make your drawings tactile. As I drew the luxuriant hair of my own collie I could remember what a joy it was to stroke him. I am told that children who read my Mister Bill and Clarence (1990, Random Century), stroke the pages. When you see a wonderful picture, say a drawing in Conté by John Skeaping RA or an oil painting by Stubbs, you can literally feel the smooth satin finish of the racehorses, and the sensitivity of their coat and skin when touched. For drawing is not only a study in anatomy, or a description of a certain character, it also gives an impression of how beautiful animals are to touch,

especially those covered in hair or fur. Heart patients are often given animals to stroke to aid recovery; not only does it slow down the heart rate but gives sensual pleasure and joy to both the person and the animal. If you are drawing creatures such as elephants, snakes, or porcupines, then stroking may not be such a sensual pleasure, and not generally advised. Yet, the act of describing the rough skin of the elephant, the prickles of the porcupine, or the smooth dryness of a snake must also involve or evoke a sensual pleasure. Describing a texture is very physical.

If you can feel deeply and passionately about the texture of animals, as Sargent expressed his pleasure at texture in materials, for example, and Stubbs obviously did with regard to horses, then your delight and love of animals and their beauty will come through in your portrayal of them.

BELOW **Stubbs studied horses and their anatomy for two years, and mastered the portrayal of their form with perfection, particularly the texture and sheen of their coats.**

DIFFERENT TEXTURES

There are certain characteristics that dictate texture to you and there are ways in which you yourself can produce the texture. The first is obviously the paper on which you are producing your image—generally the rougher the paper, the more open the lines will be between dark and light.

You should not expect fine detail in a drawing on very rough paper, especially if using charcoal, but you could draw the fleeting line of a horse or the shaggy hair of a dog or cat. The texture of your paper can dictate the medium with which you are going to draw and to some extent the subject matter. For instance, if you have rough paper, either heavyweight watercolor, sand, or pastel paper, you will draw with a broad brush, charcoal, or pastel, hoping for a more spontaneous and effective description of the animal.

The finer the paper, the more detail you can achieve. There are dozens of ways of producing texture. If you do not have a spontaneous feeling about what you want to do, then it is wiser, if you have a certain animal in mind, to try different techniques and choose the one that satisfies you the most.

Here are examples of textures of coats of animals and how the coat itself can help you choose the techniques and the materials that you use.

Do not be afraid to mix media in your trials with color and texture, but do follow the rule of always using black first if it is a broad sweep (not a line) and place the other colors on top, as in lithography. This keeps the top color brighter and clear. If you use only black line, the reverse order is appropriate. Put your color down cleanly and simply and draw in line with the black, as shown in the chapter on Monotypes on pages 101–111.

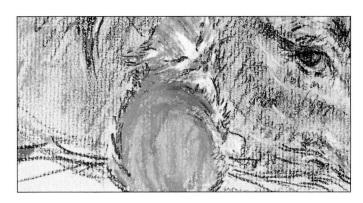

TOP Smooth charcoal on smooth paper can produce the silkiest of textures such as that of the short hair on a collie's nose.

CENTER Dry-brush is ideal for producing rougher, thicker coats and bristles, such as that of a rough-haired dog.

BOTTOM Pastels are soft and powdery and are just the thing for giving a cat lots of fluffy hair.

SHAPES

You may already be able to draw an animal standing so that you can see its legs and with its head to the left or right and body straight on (probably that is why this is the pose chosen for most commissioned portraits—it is the easiest). I hope to help you draw animals curled up, sleeping, or stretched out in positions that cover or hide some parts of their bodies that characterize them.

It is a good tip to try and completely abstractionalize the animal you are looking at. Forget that it has a head and legs and that it is a cat. Try to see it as an object making a hole in space. See what shape this hole makes in space by shutting detail out of your mind and drawing in line the shape you *see*, *not* the shape you *know* on a clean piece of paper. Try to see the inside of the hole as empty and fill in the outside, for instance the blanket on which the animal is lying, the wall behind it, or the chair leg. Fill in all this detail. Color it in if you like. Then look at the shape of the hole when you have nothing but the outside line.

Trace this line and draw the same shape onto another piece of paper. Then fill in what you see inside the hole, for instance the cat curled up, even if you cannot see its legs, head, and tail. Rely on your knowledge of the spine and what it is doing. Put in the detail and character of what you can see, the ears, the eyes, type of fur, and then place one picture over the other. You should have filled in your hole. Everything is an object in space and by describing the shape of the space outside the body, you are also describing the shape of the body within that space.

THE WAY ANIMALS MOVE

Photography has helped us understand how animals move. Before its invention, horses galloping were sometimes painted with their forelegs going out to the front and their hind legs going back at the same time, giving an unrealistic spreadeagled look to the movement of the animal. People did not understand the motion that a horse makes when galloping because it was too quick to see.

Photography has enabled us to understand what happens at speed. We now know that cats turn when falling so that they can land on their feet. Before drawing an animal you should watch carefully how it moves, by observing what type of animal it is, and the character of the animal itself. Of course, although all cats are agile, there are some fat, lazy cats who do not move quite as quickly as thin slinky ones. A cart horse is a delight to

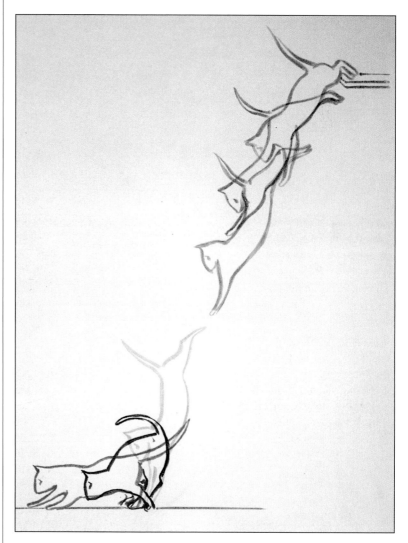

ᴀʙᴏᴠᴇ **Cats are amazingly lithe, and can jump from considerable heights without harming themselves. This diagram shows how the cat uses its** body, muscles, and agility to compensate for the fall, and to be sure of a safe landing.

see unharnessed and let loose in a paddock for this heavy creature will gambol, jump, and run and be very skittish and playful. But it is still a heavy cart horse doing all this, so the animal will have the characteristic movements of a cart horse gamboling and jumping, which is very different from a thoroughbred let out into the paddock, whose movements, because of its longer legs and more refined shape, will be much more graceful.

Stiller animals are easier to draw for the beginner, so it is better to start with those that sleep a lot such as cats and dogs, or if you are going to the zoo, elephants, which are so large they do not move a great deal and giraffes, which also make good subjects. Domestic animals tend to come back into the same positions time and time again, though they may not keep them for long. If you are drawing from life it is a good idea to have two or three drawings going at once that you can return to, putting in the details of color and markings by what you know about the animal and being able to go back and have another look if need be.

Worrying about movement only applies if you are drawing from life. But the *understanding* of how and why an animal moves in a particular way is essential to bring life to works done from a photograph.

RIGHT, TOP TO BOTTOM When drawing from life, it is a good idea to do several quick sketches first, ensuring that you capture the position and likeness of the subject. You can always fill in details later.

CHARACTER

Every animal has its own character and each of us perceives that character differently. This aspect is close to our hearts; for instance I have an 18-year-old brindle female cat with large green eyes whose favorite spot is the corner of the kitchen table and who winks at people if they wink at her. She has been described diversely as an ill-tempered old bag, a witch's cat, and a most beautiful creature, depending on whether the speaker likes her or not or feels an affinity with her or, more importantly, whether she likes them. Cats can be portrayed as witches' familiars, or fluffy little creatures; some people are afraid of cats and can never really see them in a good light.

Many people are happier with dogs, especially men. So dog portraits and drawings of dogs show them in a very good light, as splendid, courageous, loving creatures—which they are, of course.

For an animal portrait, it is of the utmost importance to talk to the owner and listen to how he or she feels about their pet. You must find out about the pet's character because it will not matter how well you have drawn or painted the color of its fur if you have not caught that essence that makes it not just a spaniel, a poodle, or a fluffy cat but *that* person's spaniel, poodle, or fluffy cat.

After line, character is all, in drawing animals. They do not wear clothes or paint their faces or wear hats or carry identifying objects such as canes or cigars, and with animals covered in fur you cannot see as much of their facial expression as you can with human beings and other naked animals, so you have to look for things to emphasize. The overall line must be very strong. My line and my drawing as a whole has to describe my old cat, Miss Emma, with her thin bones, her frail body, her determination and her right as an old cat to be on the corner of the table she has chosen as her special place, and her relationship to me, the person she loves. She is not just any old cat sitting on the corner of a table, but *my* old cat sitting on the corner of the table.

The better you know an animal, the more there will be to convey in the drawing. You will see signs of age, character, and temperament, that are only visible after time.

Portraits of dogs are the most common throughout the history of animal portraiture. This is largely because they have been regarded as "man's best friend," and as a result are seen as showing such emotions as loyalty, mourning, and protection. Portraits vary considerably, however, depending on the desired effect of the painting. Here are a few examples.

ABOVE **Miss Emma, pen; Kay Gallwey**

ABOVE *Hounds*, acrylic; Michael Kitchen-Hurle

And as he gazed the purpose of Corrigan Ban
gleamed in his eyes

ABOVE *Corrigan Ban*, pencil; K. F. Barker

ABOVE *There's No Place Like Home*, Edwin Landseer

LEFT *Tinkerbell*, pencil; K. F. Barker

And "Damaged goods" accused Rebecca's sad reproachful eyes.

ABOVE *Rebecca*, pencil; K. F. Barker

"Tex"
Stephen Crowther
29th Jan. 1990

ABOVE *Tex*, charcoal, Conté, and pastel; Stephen Crowther

ABOVE *Fox, acrylic; Michael Kitchen-Hurle*

ABOVE *The Old Shepherd's Chief Mourner*, Edwin Landseer

INDIVIDUAL FEATURES

Horses' Noses

a. Shire

b. Shetland stallion

c. Shagya Arab

d. Arab stallion

Facial features and limbs change dramatically from animal to animal, even from breed to breed. Simply by taking a few examples of cat, dog, and horse, one can see that their individual features are extremely unique.

Dogs' Noses

a. Terrier

b. Collie

c. Bulldog

Cats' Eyes and Noses

a. British Shorthair

b. Peke-faced Persian

c. Young Burmese

d. Modern Persian

INDIVIDUAL FEATURES

Horses' Feet

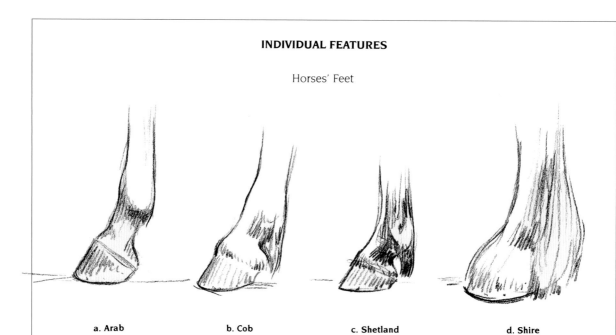

a. Arab   b. Cob   c. Shetland   d. Shire

Dogs' Feet

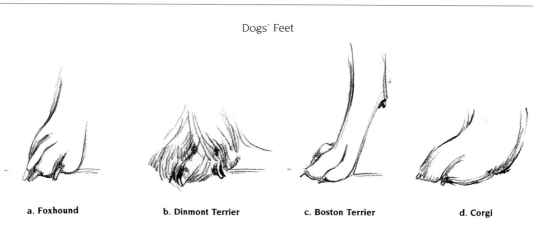

a. Foxhound   b. Dinmont Terrier   c. Boston Terrier   d. Corgi

Cats' Feet

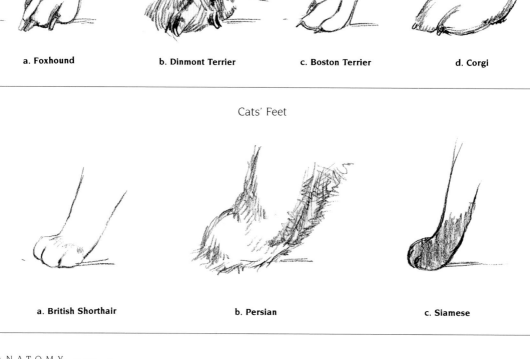

a. British Shorthair   b. Persian   c. Siamese

3
FORM AND PERSPECTIVE

It is time now to see how the shape of an
animal is affected when viewed from different angles
and distances. We all know that objects look different
depending on the angle, how far away they are,
whether they are moving away from or toward the
viewer, or whether they are being seen from above or
below the viewer. Drawing in perspective is to put
down what you see and not what you think should be
seen. Perception is not a simple matter. Our eye can
be misled by the workings of our brain. Human
beings need to structure objects they see into shapes
and patterns that make sense to them.

FORESHORTENING

We know a horse's leg is long, so when we draw it we tend to draw it as we know it and not as we see it. A bent leg, or one viewed from in front, appears shorter and distorted. The mind tries to minimize this apparent distortion and restores the leg as closely as possible to a leg viewed flat on. The artist's aim, after lots of practice, is to be able to believe what you see, then draw it with enough conviction to communicate to other people what you have seen.

Foreshortening is when something comes toward you and recedes. If I stand in front of you and point my finger at you, my arm will be seen from a foreshortened angle. If you sit in front of somebody across a room their body will be upright, but you will see their legs at a foreshortened angle. However you look at an object, some part of it must be foreshortened. Because it is a solid object in space, some part must always be farthest away and some part nearest to you. We must try and find ways of explaining this in our drawings. When a cat is lying down sleeping the part toward you will be bigger and have sharper detail. This is describing space on a flat surface with an object in it.

We are trying to create a sense of depth, of a background, a middle, and a foreground in our picture. The trees in the foreground are larger and more detailed, for instance, while the trees, and the road and fence get smaller and blurred as they recede.

Drawing a bulky figure such as a bear, cat, or dog lying down is fairly easy when compared to the difficulties posed when the animal is standing up, especially if it has long and complicated legs, like a horse or giraffe.

BELOW **In this cave painting, conveying the perspective accurately has proved difficult for the artist. He is familiar with the animal and so can portray it in perspective. Yet, when it comes to adding the arrows that wounded it, the perspective is lost.**

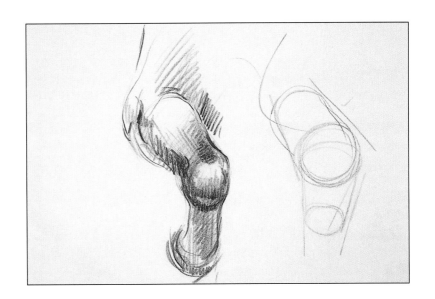

RIGHT, TOP TO BOTTOM **By using a series of ellipses, one at each joint, you can attempt to draw the foreshortened leg or arm in perspective and in proportion.**

ABOVE Every time you attempt to draw an animal, there will be a part of it that is in the background. Although it is often difficult, you must be able to portray this accurately in order to make your picture convincing. You may feel that the end nearest to you is disproportionately large, but this must be overcome in order to depict the animal correctly.

ABOVE It is normal to expect the foreground to be sharper and have more detail than the background. It is how we see things in every walk of life, and the same should therefore be applied to drawing.

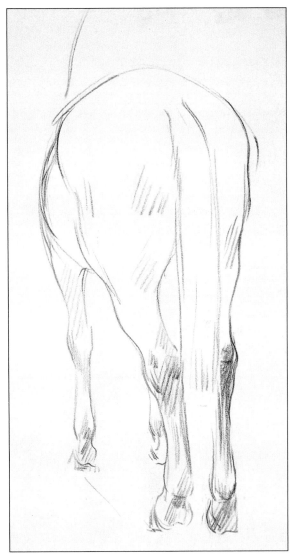

Foreshortening of these legs can seem daunting to a beginner, but again your knowledge of the skeleton can help. My main advice is always to watch your subject for some time before attempting to draw. Try to understand how it stands and the movements it makes. A cat or dog will lie down to rest, while other animals like horses, cows, or elephants will constantly shift their weight from one leg to the other to give each leg some rest. In your drawing you must show how this weight is distributed. Note how the spine and hip angle changes with the shifting of this weight. Remember that however large a horse or elephant is, the legs farther away must, of course, be smaller and the near ones larger and sharper in detail.

Shadows emphasize depth in a picture, especially in drawing rather than painting where you have more pattern and color in the picture to help you achieve depth.

Let us take the head of a cat, and see it as an object in space using perspective and foreshortening.

ABOVE LEFT **A standing horse will have a very even, balanced distribution of weight. Once it moves, this weight will of course shift in order to compensate for this change of posture. This is true of all animals when they move and joints, limbs, and muscles will look very different as a result.**

ABOVE RIGHT **No matter how large an animal is, there will always be a part of it that is farther away and must therefore be drawn smaller to meet proportion and perspective requirements.**

USING SHAPES TO DRAW PERSPECTIVE

Confining the head in a box shape will give you a frame to work in. Draw the box in line, then see how the features fit in. The same technique can be used for any animal, or human beings for that matter.

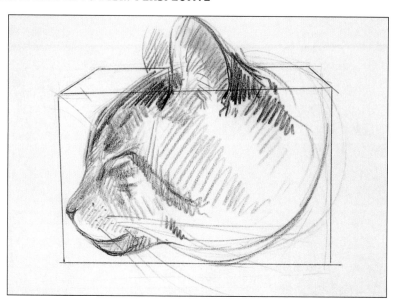

We have to see the cat's head as a shape that fits into a box—four sides and a top and bottom. Many people draw cats as if they only have a front to the head, flat like a pansy. They forget that some of a cat's head is also behind the ears, and so in some ways rather similar to a human being. This drawing shows my daughter from the side

and front. If you trace the cat's face and lay it over the drawing of my daughter you can see this. They both have large eye sockets, a broad top to the head, and small chin. Human beings and cats see to the front and sides in one go, unlike dogs, horses, and all animals that have noses that protrude from the skull forming a block between the eyes, so making them see differently. Long-nosed dogs and horses, for instance, have to turn their heads to see forward.

LEFT It is always helpful to be able to put the subject into general shapes, and in this drawing of a horse, I have tried to simplify the shapes. You can do this with all animals.

THE EYELINE

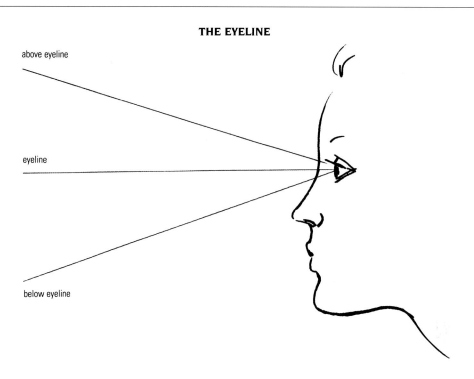

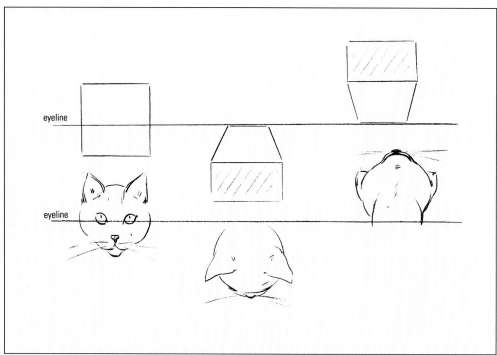

Artists speak of an object being above or below the eyeline. Anything on the eyeline is on a level with your eyes; and anything above or below the eyeline will change in perspective and proportion (above).

4

LINE AND MOVEMENT, LIGHT AND SHADE

I am sure if you asked the Masai people to draw their cattle, they would know them in every detail because they are with them constantly. In general we are mostly concerned with domestic animals because we live with them day by day. So if you want to draw an animal you are not with every day, it is better to equip yourself with some knowledge of how it moves and why it moves as it does.

A horse, for instance, has very little free lateral body movement. Its head and neck have to balance its body. The head level changes with movement, going up and down *and* backward and forward.

MOVEMENT

Animals always show to advantage what kind they are and their own special beauty when they are executing the movements their bodies were built to perform. If you look at a horse galloping and jumping, which it is built to do, it is very beautiful. The cat, on the other hand, is built for climbing, springing, stretching, and very flexible movement. If you compare cats and horses lying down, you will see, as I have said, that the horse is awkward, although it makes a beautiful shape when it is finally lying down, whereas a cat has a graceful ability to lie and stretch on anything from the floor to tree trunks. Remember the pictures you have seen of panthers or lions looped gracefully over large branches of trees.

Notice differences between the elbows, knees, and ankles in the human skeleton, as compared with those in the skeleton of an animal because of their different ways of

ABOVE Early paintings like this, dating back as far as c.1400 B.C., often show extreme accuracy in the portrayal of animals. Invariably this accuracy is the result of great familiarity with the animals—either as those that are hunted, or those used for work.

ABOVE, LEFT, AND BELOW **Large** and heavy animals like the horse and the rhinoceros do not look comfortable lying down. The rhino is heavy and looks clumsy once he has managed to do it. As with the horse, the actual task of lying down looks arduous and even painful. Cats, on the other hand, seem to lie down effortlessly at every given opportunity, and always looks cozy and comfortable.

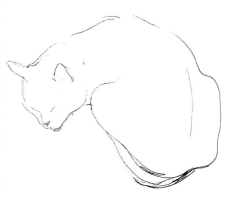

ABOVE Horse galloping, line and mocha.

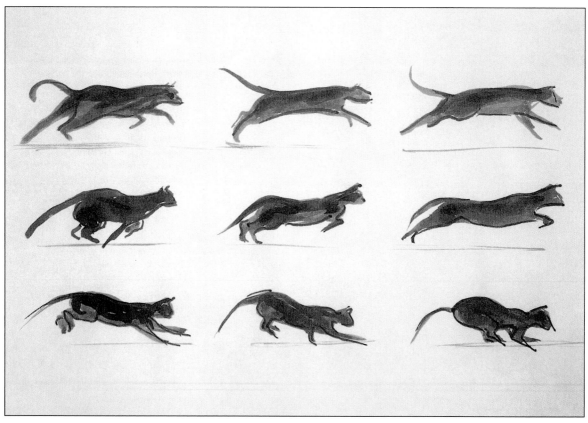

ABOVE Cat running, line and mocha.

walking. This will help you understand where the limbs bend and how they balance themselves and explains why they make the movements they do. Look at the drawings of a dog from standing to galloping (pages 56–57), and imagine the skeleton inside the dog. The faster the dog goes, the longer it stretches out. Try to see this line of movement; it will help get balance and feeling into your drawings, and will help you recognize the basic shape. Compare this with the movement of a cat, a horse, and an elephant (left and right).

The only animal that does not change its head level when galloping is the giraffe because it has to balance and support its head weight against its body, which gives it a curiously graceful movement.

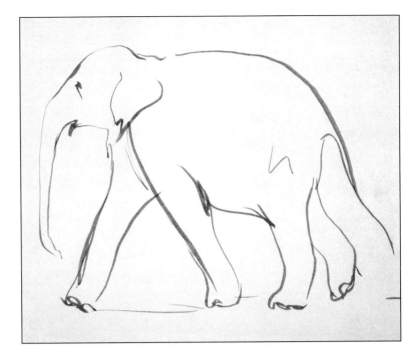

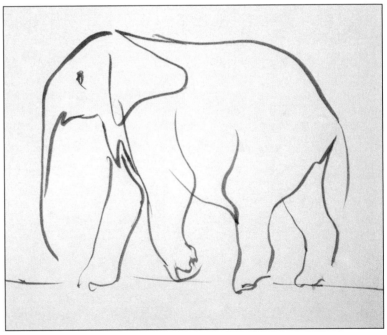

TOP AND ABOVE **Two drawings illustrate the line of a walking elephant.**

IDENTIFYING LINE OF MOVEMENT

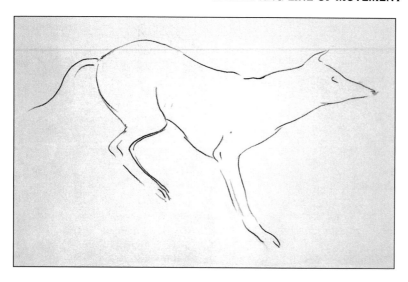

An effective way of doing this is to put a piece of tracing paper onto pictures or photographs. Then take a felt-tip pen and draw a line where you think the main line of movement in the animal is. Do practice this, as it will help a lot; even when you do not have a pencil and paper in front of you, train yourself to see this line in everything you look at. It will be a great help for you in describing, in drawing, the movements of animals.

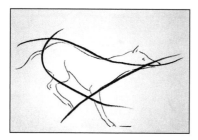

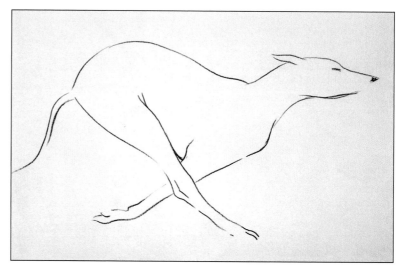

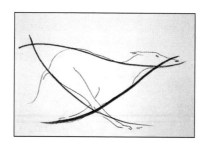

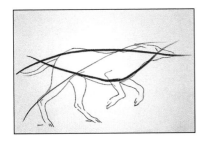

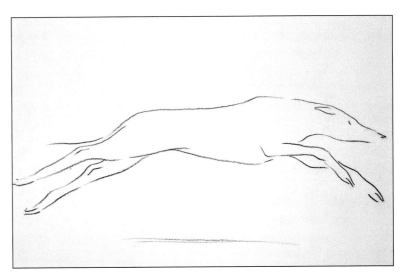

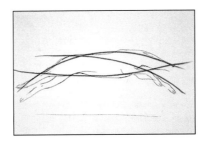

LINE AND MOVEMENT

Because this book is about drawing animals that move, unlike plants, still life, or landscape, or designs for textiles and wallpaper, we have to find some way of describing our subjects on paper so that they are not a motif but real living creatures.

Unless blessed with extreme luck when your cat or dog is lying still for a while, drawing animals from life is inevitably restricted in time. It is most important to work as quickly as possible, putting down the main line and characteristics, with the essentials first and working on the details later.

Before you actually start a drawing, as well as watching and getting to know your subject, it also helps, before your first initial powerful lines, to practice drawing individual parts of the animal—the eyes, ears, paws, or small sections of the coat or fur color—trying to get them right in absolute detail.

These studies can be referred to later on when the animal has moved. You will find you can learn to memorize them and you can use them in other pictures as well.

When doing your swift sketch on which you are going to base your final drawing work smoothly and quickly, but without haste or panic. Remember, animals often come back to the same position. You can, of course, use photography in conjunction with your sketches.

LIGHT AND SHADE

There are many ways of describing forms in space. The most difficult is pure line. If you look at Picasso's line drawings, or Matisse's blue cutouts, you will understand that a great artist, or perhaps a naive one (such as a line drawing done by a small child) can achieve by line, and line alone, the full extent of what he is trying to express and describe "proportion," perspective, weight, character, and form in space, in this one single line.

For a beginner this is very difficult to achieve. Also we are concerned with drawing animals mostly covered in hair, unlike Picasso's and Matisse's nudes. We are trying to find the best way to draw our pets or other animals in pencil, chalks, watercolor, or wash and line. Later we will see under Sketchbooks on pages 112–117 how a single line can describe an animal's shape and character. Here we consider how best we can achieve this by the use of light and shade.

I am not discussing a drawing where you have no power over the light, as with sketching an animal moving in a field or zoo, but a thought-out picture drawn at home.

ABOVE AND OPPOSITE **Depending on where your subject is in relation to the light, whether it is natural or set up by you, the effects of light and shade will be different every time, and a mixture of shapes and textures will be dominant whether in shadow or highlighted. Line and smudge is a particularly effective way of achieving the subtleties of light and shade.**

First decide where you are going to place your subject in relation to the light. This will give you shadows and gradations of tone. Consider what type of feeling you want in the picture—bright and cheerful? dark and dramatic? Think of the character of the animal if it is a portrait, or the tale you wish to tell if you are illustrating a theme. The lighting you choose will determine the atmosphere of the picture. If you are using natural light, remember it changes quickly with time, so your shadows will move (unless you are using a photographic reference). Light on a subject explains its shape. You must always see the shadows on and around an animal as something alive and moving, not just a flat dark surface.

You should be able to see into and through shadows. Beginners

ABOVE **John Skeaping showed a great understanding of animals and their anatomy. In this pen and charcoal drawing he uses light and shade to give the reedbuck texture, form and character.**

often have trouble with drawing shadows on patterns or different colors, such as a black and white cat or a horse with dark mane and tail. This is difficult to help you with in words alone, so I have tried to explain it in drawing (see pages 58–59). You will see how light and shade can describe the texture and sheen of an animal's coat. Try practicing doing small samples of coats, an eye or an ear, without trying always for a full drawing of the animal.

Light is essential to the atmosphere of the picture. Consider Rembrandt's small picture St. Jerome

in the Dark painted in 1642. There is very little light in the picture and the whole atmosphere is very dark in tone. Try putting a piece of white paper next to the picture, then relate the lightness of the paper to the tone of the picture. The small amount of light that is streaming in through the windows tells you the complete story and creates a unique atmosphere.

The 19th-century French Impressionists were obsessed by light, trying to describe the feeling and quality of the sun, its effect on objects, and the beauty of the shadows it made. Because we are drawing and not painting, we will use charcoal, soft pencils, Conté in black, sanguine, and white, pastels and line with ink or watercolor wash, watercolor line, and other techniques to describe light and shade on our subjects.

COMPOSITION AND LAYOUT

Composition is how a picture is constructed and what its formation is when put together and placed on a sheet of paper. It is an artificial way of arranging your objects or subjects together to make a seemingly natural picture in a way that is harmonious to the onlooker. Are you drawing a portrait of a racehorse, or are you illustrating a herd of elephants? Painting the local dog show or filling a page with sketches of a moving kitten? Whatever you are doing, there are certain basic rules.

If you are drawing a portrait, you need to place the animal in the middle of the picture, taking up most of the space and showing its most flattering features. Anything positioned around it (for example, trees or a dog basket) should emphasize the importance of the subject you are putting on display, not detract from it. So all shapes surrounding it should draw the eye to the main subject of your picture.

The picture should not "lead off" to the right or the left. The viewer should not feel as if the dog, for instance, is sinking through the floor or taking off into the top of the picture. The eye should be happy with what it sees because of the arrangement of the objects; they should appear correct.

In these Victorian pictures of groups of animals (opposite), especially the terriers in the country, we see the artist has cleverly detailed the animals themselves but left the background simply sketched in; so in no way does the eye detract from the dogs themselves. If you are drawing a portrait with little or no background you need to place the animal on the page describing it fully, including its size, shape, and character. Leave enough space around it, but not so much that it appears to float. When mounting a picture for framing, framers often have a standing rule for good mounts, for example leaving an edge of 3in. on three sides and 4in. at the bottom. If you have

ABOVE The dog is the subject of this drawing, and the basket is there merely to emphasize this. There is no further background, which can quite often dominate a drawing, leading to a detraction from the subject.

"A serene softly breathing heap."

"Tinker Bell stared upwards."

composed your picture well but it is overlapping or very near the edge of the paper a good framer will adjust the proportions for you when mounting the work.

When you first start drawing it is best to keep your compositions as simple as possible, but it is worth looking at how established artists have tackled the problem of composition. The Viennese Secessionist painter Gustav Klimt, who painted on square canvases, often constructed his pictures with heads right up to the top of the picture or even a little out, but the way he placed his sitters on the canvas and the pose they took were thought out carefully and well composed. In the Degas picture *Day at the Races* the artist employs a complicated technique. The horses are going off the edge of the picture, but because of the brilliant color, light, and excitement, the composition works. The arrangement makes you want to lean into the frame and see what is happening either side of the picture; it is like looking through a window into a different world. This technique can also be seen in his other paintings; the way he positions his dancers, for example, gives extreme excitement to the picture and creates a feeling of life going on in another world outside the picture plane. This takes courage and a world of knowledge.

ABOVE *Dinah*, pencil; K. F. Barker

LEFT *Tinkerbell*, pencil; K. F. Barker

THE FOCAL POINT

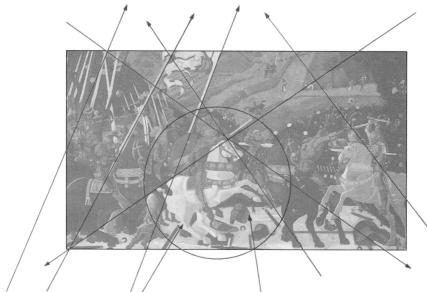

In *The Rout of San Romano* by Uccello, you can see how the artist has arranged the spears and lances held by the horsemen and the pattern of the horses' legs to point a way to lead you into the picture.

So, if you are drawing a gymkhana or a group activity, you will need structure in the picture as in the Uccello to hold it together and indicate to those looking at the picture what is relevant.

LAYOUT

Having chosen your subject, you must organize its elements according to what you are going to draw. Consider first the gymkhana or the group animal picture. Take a sheet of paper and all your references. If the picture is a landscape shape, draw a number of landscape-shaped boxes on the sheet of paper.

Make up your mind what is to be your focal point and what the picture is about. Determine the time of day, the light, and the atmosphere and find what will help you illustrate this in your reference.

ABOVE Two preliminary stages in a drawing of horses in a field. Note in the first drawing (top) that the eye level runs through all of the horses just below the top of the neck, ensuring that all horses are represented as being the same size. The next stage (bottom) is to decide where the light is coming from; in this case, from the top left-hand corner. This allows some of the horses to be in shadow, almost in silhouette and other horses to be well lit along the flank. The foliage in the background has been shown in shadow which allows the backs of the horses to be clearly marked. The fence gives a sense of perspective depth. From here, the drawing could be elaborated further to include, for example, farm buildings if desired.

Decide how far away you want what is happening to be, and if you need anything important in the foreground. If you have something big, such as a person or a horse, the rest of the picture must relate to this and describe from how far away the viewer is looking. Do several scale sketches in your boxes, drawing the skyline and placing the subject or subjects where you think they would be most interesting. Use light and shade, color, or objects to point the attention of your viewer toward the main focus of the picture.

If you are drawing a portrait within a landscape, then you need to use your boxes again. Place the figure in the middle to its greatest advantage and build a landscape around that enhances it and does not intrude on the subject, that is if you need anything at all. Quite often drawings of animals do not even use much of a background. Even in pictures such as Landseer's *Monarch of the Glen*, which is a huge picture, most of the picture is dark, atmospheric, and wild, and the light picks up only the single, expertly placed stag. Landseer has achieved perfect composition by using light and dark as Rembrandt did in his picture of *St. Jerome in the Dark*.

CONCERNING COLOR

I shall discuss color here because later I shall look at using colored chalks and pastels, but as this book is only about drawing I shall not consider color as used in painting, that is the mixing of and techniques of oil paints or acrylics. Pencils, crayons, chalk, and pastels alone are wonderful media for showing the life, movement, and beauty of animals.

As it is not necessary to use a huge array of color, for animals do not wear clothes, shoes, and hats, so your subject will be in different tones of the same color (for example, a brown dog) if you are using pastels or maybe a little of other colors. It is best to keep it very simple, especially for beginners. It is also helpful for

BELOW Simple use of color can have bold results. Just one color used to great effect can often be more successful than using several.

beginners, as well as being a most attractive way of drawing, to work on colored paper. There is nothing more daunting to start with than a black pencil and a large piece of white paper. A smooth texture is better for drawing as a rough paper is more difficult to handle and it is less easy to use the eraser, though you should stay away from the eraser as much as possible.

A good combination is to use beige or buff-colored paper of a smooth texture, with three colors of Conté—sanguine, black, and white. This can achieve a lovely effect and something that will look more like a finished picture than if you had done the same subject on white paper. When you have mastered this technique, you can gradually start to add color; use beiges, pinks, creams, and yellows to work with the Conté. These light shades will show up on the tinted paper and the tinted paper will in turn fill in as a background to your drawing. Try using blues where you would normally use black.

Then you can begin to work in pastels and to undertake and use more complex and difficult techniques, bringing in both light and shade and tone value using color. The same techniques can be applied to watercolor, that is

ABOVE Drawing on colored paper is often a good idea. Not only will it produce very satisfying results, but it is also less daunting than trying to fill the large gaps that always appear on white paper.

starting with black, sanguine, and body color or white on tinted paper and gradually bringing in different colors to describe the same lines and shapes. In this way you can build up your confidence and not take on too much until you are more practiced, thus avoiding discouragement at an early stage when you are still learning rather than producing serious work.

6

PENCIL AND CHARCOAL

Pencil and charcoal are popular media for drawing animals, particularly for sketching. Pencil will give you sharp detail for finer sketches, whereas charcoal allows for a strong, bold image.

USING PENCILS

Pencils, unlike pens, can vary the lightness and darkness of the line according to the pressure and stroke of the pencil or charcoal. A pen, depending on the nib you are using, may get broader or thinner, but will always have the same intensity and darkness, rather like an etching, while pencils or charcoal can go from the palest of pale to the very darkest of dark in one line. You might argue that this can also be done with a brush and ink or brush and watercolor. This is true but, with a pencil especially, one has absolute control. With pencil and charcoal, unlike watercolor, wash and inks, you can eradicate any mistakes with putty rubber or bread and have totally different techniques from these media as well.

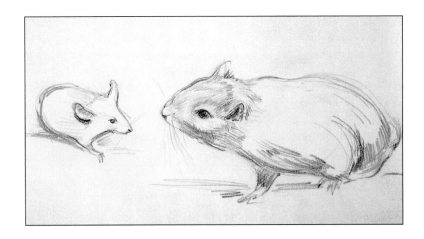

Although often frowned upon, the humble pencil, in my opinion, the softer the better (because of this flexibility of line and tone), is the best possible medium for learning to draw. With this medium, even if you go on to watercolor or pastels, you have between your fingertips the chance to explore all

ABOVE **Pencil can be used to simple effect, and is well suited to the portrayal of the fine hair and whiskers of this mouse and hamster.**

BELOW **Pencil is most effective when conveying the textures and colorings of fur. Together with the white chalk marks, the exact patterns of these two cats have been shown, with simple pencil lines.**

possibilities. From sketchbook to finished drawings, pencil and charcoal offer a full range of tone, line, and texture by themselves. When faced with a pencil, or a piece of charcoal, and a piece of white paper, people tend to get frightened and diversify into other media such as chalks, pastels, watercolors, or oils, long before they have got the hang of this essential and beautiful medium.

Conté is a mixture of clay, graphite, water, and paste, hardened by baking in a kiln, then later pressed into wood. This was the beginning of modern pencils. Conté is available in black, sepia, and sanguine and other earth colors of Conté pencils are made from kaolin, waxes, and dyes. Look to people like Augustus John and Degas to see the sheer beauty of this type of drawing. onte came later.

ABOVE In contrast to the fine lines of the mice (page 69) the broad lines of a soft pencil have captured this old ram's very character. He is big and shaggy, and keeps a constant watchful eye on everything that goes on.

RIGHT Conté crayon has been used on its side to give the stylish, angular shapes that form this nesting mouse and his home. This method suits some animals extremely well—for example the gazelles on page 67.

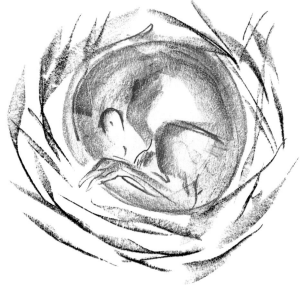

USING CHARCOAL

Charcoal is the oldest medium, and is literally burnt wood. This is the medium with which prehistoric cavemen drew on the walls of their caves. They used a combination of charred bones, sticks, and soot from their fires as well as vegetable dyes and earth. It is a very easy material to cover large surfaces with. Charcoal can be smudged, rubbed out, or added to. You can draw with it in wild sweeps or make careful drawings with the subtlest of lines. It smudges easily, however, and for a beginner can be difficult as it can become messy.

It is better for the beginner to use compressed charcoal; that is, small sticks of charcoal 3–4in. long, which do not break as easily as charcoal sticks and can be sharpened, although they are less easy to rub out and you cannot use the technique of picking out, described below, with bread or putty as you can with looser-grained charcoal sticks, so easily.

Then there are charcoal pencils, which are even less messy and better for small-scale, or detailed, work. As the charcoal is in a pencil form, however, you cannot use it as you can stick or compressed charcoals, where the whole and sides of the surface can be used to make different textures.

Charcoal is a flexible medium. You can spread charcoal with a stump. You can graduate the tone and use it with wash. Powdered charcoal, from sharpening any of these three charcoals, can be used to draw or make textures with your fingers, by itself, or with a rag or with cotton wool. You can lay down charcoal, using it as a broad surface, then pick it off with a putty rubber for highlights. Use bread rolled into soft pellets if you have run out of putty rubber.

Because it can be removed by blowing, or dusting off with chamois leather or a piece of soft material, charcoal can be used in conjunction with pastels, either for preliminary drawing or as a drawing medium. It is also good for drawing on canvas before beginning an oil painting as you can work the

BELOW Charcoal is fantastic for capturing the exact look of hair, fur and coats of animals. It is amazing to see how the effects can vary even when using the same medium. The shagginess of the terrier, created using charcoal on its side, is contrasted with the silkiness of the collie (page 72).

painting out in charcoal, changing it as you go, then dusting off to leave marks sufficient to guide the painting, but not fixed enough to show through the paint.

Charcoal can be used on any type of paper. The rougher the paper, the rougher the line because charcoal is a medium that reveals the quality of the paper more than any other. Compressed charcoal probably works better with smoother surfaces, whereas sticks work well on prominent grain. Charcoal, worked with white chalk, is extremely effective on tinted paper. It is a wonderful medium for drawing animals, but a medium that a beginner should be wary of, as it can deteriorate into a mess if you do not know what you are doing. Always keep your lines simple and free with charcoal. It is not a medium for cross-hatching and fine detail unless you are using sharpened charcoal pencil.

BELOW The fur of this collie was achieved through picking off charcoal with a putty rubber. Compare the fur with that of the terrier (page 71). They both have soft and smooth hair, but you know instinctively that they feel very different from one another.

ELEPHANT
BLACK CONTÉ AND WHITE CHALK
DRAWING ON TINTED PAPER

I did this drawing from sketches in the zoo and from what I had in my head, as I have drawn elephants quite a lot. They have marvelous character, are kind and funny animals, and make lovely shapes to draw.

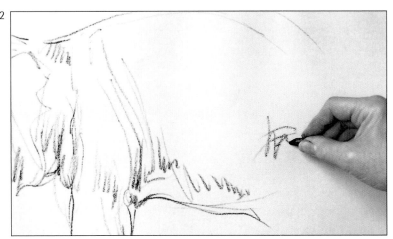

1 First, I simply looked. Then I swung into the drawing with energy. If this one was not right I could do another. I put the main lines in, checking proportion as I drew.

2 Remember, however big and bulky an elephant looks, the viewer must see the skeleton underneath. Note how long his front legs are and how the belly slopes down to the back legs. I tried to describe how bony the big head is compared with the loose-skinned back legs and rump.

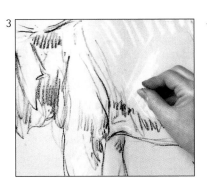

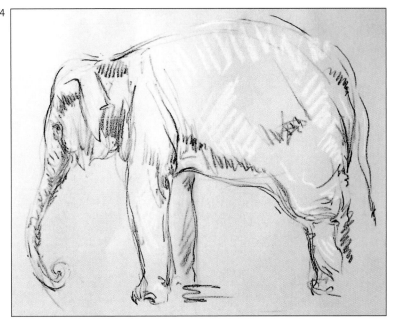

3 White chalk was used to bring out the shape and describe the rough texture of the skin.

4 I did not want to overdo the drawing. I felt I had got all I had to say about the elephant down on paper, then left it.

GAZELLES
BLACK, WHITE, AND RUST CONTÉ CRAYON
ON TINTED PAPER

Drawing lively animals like these needs a great deal of observation. I have many drawings of gazelles in my sketchbook and now have the animals in my head. So I could draw this picture without reference. Try doing this yourself; it is very good training for your memory and once you have committed the shape of an animal to your mind you can draw it any time without reference.

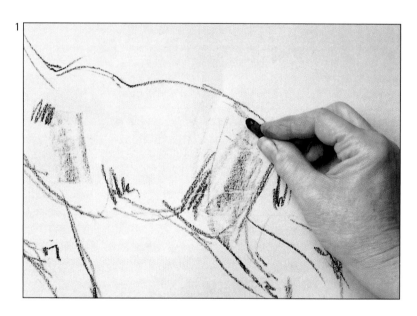

1 When I had thought about the picture and what I wanted from it I set to, getting the line down quick and strong. I used the sharpened end of the black Conté to draw the main shapes.

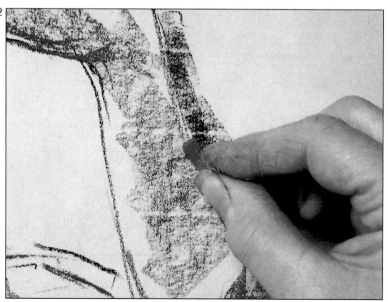

2 Here I used the rust Conté on its side; I broke it in two to make it shorter and drew with it in broad sweeps following the shape of the animal, pressing down hard where it should be darker and less hard where it should be lighter. I also used the black Conté in the same way to provide the base for the mane.

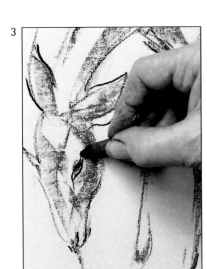

3 A little of the black Conté used on its point defined the neck and underbelly. I also used the point for the eyes, ears, and mane.

4 Very quickly, I picked out the white markings on the gazelles' coats with white chalk.

5 I was happy with the finished drawing. Once you have achieved your object, do not play around with it and spoil it, but learn to leave it.

7
PEN OR BRUSH
AND INK

As you are drawing animals and not a static subject such as a still life or flowers, you need to have a different attitude toward pen, ink, and wash. If you are drawing a moving animal, it is best to set yourself up with a smooth paper watercolor block or spiral-bound sketchbook, the types of nib pens or fiber-tipped pens and brushes you are going to work with, either black or sanguine-colored ink, two pots of water, and a small plastic or china palette.

Sometimes it is better for the amateur artist to lay down a wash first and use the pen afterward, then work on the drawing again using a brush for texture.

USING PEN OR BRUSH AND INK

The bold line of a pen, although many amateurs are reluctant to use it, can be exciting to use and produce very lively pictures if used with flair. The outcome depends on the nib or the point you are using. I think there is nothing better than two or three different size good-quality black fiber-tipped pens and sketchbook if you are drawing live animals, particularly at the zoo. There are many sizes of fiber-tipped pens that are great for quick drawing. This medium can always be used in conjunction with smudged chalk, which creates the same effect as a wash.

The finer the pen nib, the more intricate the drawing can be. There are many techniques such as cross-hatching and modeling with the pen that can be used to build up a detailed picture. This technique is

best used on a picture built up from references, sketches, and photographs, so that you can sketch the outline of the picture in pencil once you have the subject and composition. Then get to work on it afterward in ink to produce detailed form and depth; it is better to keep this work for later at home under controlled circumstances.

ABOVE **With pen and wash you can achieve the finer details of the animal's shape and characteristics without losing the liveliness of the drawing.**

BELOW **This is a straightforward example of ink and wash using a brush. The fluidity of the tiger's movements is accentuated by the flow of the wash.**

Wash can be used in these more intricate pictures, but must be placed exactly on the paper. You must think out the composition thoroughly and do a rough in pencil beforehand so that it can be rubbed out afterward. Pen takes time, unlike other more relaxed pictures that you can produce more spontaneously and with a quicker result. Pen can also be used under, over the top of, and in conjunction with, watercolors as well as ink and wash.

ABOVE **Using line and wash you can keep drawings very simple and delicate. The wash is used to depict light and shade, and the more intricate details have been added with a pen.**

PAPER

For wash, or line and wash unless you are using a block, it is wise to strap your paper down to your drawing board with masking tape to ensure it does not buckle. The more wash you put on, the more the paper has a tendency to buckle.

Tinted watercolor paper can be bought, on which you can use line, wash and body color (gouache), or charcoal and white Conté to highlight the wash. It is possible to

use "rough" good quality paper strapped down and achieve an excellent effect with wash and line. This is not a good method for a detailed drawing, though the effect of the broken line that will be forced on you by the roughness or grain of the paper will produce lively work.

BELOW **Some of the many different types of watercolor paper available.**

FARMYARD ANIMALS

Here, Richard Bell demonstrated that pen and ink is a effective medium for creating depth of color and texture of fur and feathers.

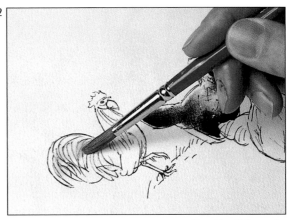

1 The artist draws a very basic outline of the chickens in pen and ink. Once the subject is drawn, the artist adds minimal background to give the picture depth and perspective.

2 The artist then moves from pen to brush. He adds a light wash to the bodies of the chickens.

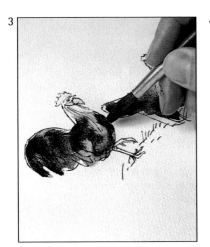

3 Ink is added, again with a brush and is used to give the bodies texture and color. The tones vary according to the effects of light and shade.

4 In a similar way, the background is elaborated upon, and then the finer details are drawn in with a pen.

ABOVE This elephant has been drawn with a fiber-tipped pen which is great for sketches and, since it is very black, it can be used to great dramatic effect.

LEFT Using a fine-nibbed pen and wash can give much more delicate results.

TYPES OF PEN

There is an enormous range and choice of pens available. The old masters, such as Dürer or Leonardo, did wonderful work with the quill pen, but I advise the amateur to keep it as simple as possible. There are many different pens in the stores, but as you are drawing live creatures, often with luxuriant coats, you should keep your tools as broad and easy as you can.

You can find many variations of the fiber-tip pen from very fine to very broad that will suit any work you undertake. It is best not to confuse yourself with too large a variety to begin with, but keep in mind that the important thing is the drawing itself and the final picture you will produce. You can get waylaid with a lot of fancy nibs and different types of pens used normally only by graphic artists or architects and end up with an overworked and boring drawing. Prehistoric cave dwellers originally drew with charcoal sticks from the fire and they produced amazing pictures. Your medium must come second to your ability and to your joy in drawing.

Inks, of course, are wonderful to use with brush as well as pen. A good fine sable or Chinese brush, of maybe one or two different thicknesses, and a wash, are easier to use than a pen, but still constrict you to a line and may give you more confidence to go into pen later.

ABOVE **Kim by Kwo Da-Wei, Chinese brush.**

COLOR

Colored inks can be marvelous in mixed media pictures, as you can find very bright inks that can be a foundation color for pastel and other media. Illustrators, such as Ernest Shephard for his *Wind in the Willows*, use pen and colored inks to great advantage and produce wonderful pictures, but it is often impossible to show or keep on the wall any of this work. It has to be kept between tissue paper in a dark place because the inks fade and the whole picture disappears eventually or turns into peculiar colors. So, unless you are willing to take this risk, it is best to keep to black and sepia. As we are talking about drawings and not finished illustrations, colored inks should only be used for mixed media experimentation, if at all.

ABOVE **It can be fun using color. You can achieve lively, abstract images using a pen and wash technique. In** order to make the drawing more life-like, simply add details in pen and ink in a single color.

8
PASTELS

Anyone who has made their own pastels will realize only too well the difficulty and vulnerability of the medium. However, they will also know that this raw pigment mixed with agacontha and stabilizer reflects light because it is made up of tiny particles, whereas the same pigment mixed with linseed oil, turpentine, and other binding agents, makes a smooth texture and does not catch the light. Many artists, including myself, hate fixing pastels for this reason but are forced to do so sometimes because if a pastel is shaken too much you will end up with half of the picture on your mount.

USING PASTELS

There are many grades and prices of pastels. The softer they come, the more brilliant the color and the more difficult to deal with. As you do not mix your colors on a palette before applying them to your paper you must find a way of placing each individual color next to another to create the same effect. Because of this juxtaposition, of opposing colors to produce a desired effect, you will have a totally different look from an oil painting, a shimmering effect that can only be achieved by pastels.

Again, the amateur should not become too carried away by the sheer number and brilliance of pastels to be seen in an art store. There is time enough for that. To start with I suggest you choose a smallish box of good (because it is never wise to use inferior materials), but not too expensive, pastels. You can always buy a few single very soft pastels for practice, but if you begin with a whole box of top-grade soft pastels you will find you have not only spent a fortune but are going to be in a mess.

Control of your medium is all-important. Once down on paper it is possible, with either a putty rubber or bread, to get pastel off again, but it will smudge the outline and often leave a mark and take the life of the drawing away. Luckily you can fix the mark and use more pastel on top if you really have to.

Beginners should place their colors on the paper as clearly and distinctly as possible. There are a number of techniques to use, but rubbing, smudging, and lifting should be kept to a minimum. Degas used a brilliant technique in some parts of his pictures of putting the pastel down in a block, spraying this with skimmed milk, leaving it to dry to form a solid base, then working lightly on top again, with more pastel, producing a chalky and light-catching effect. It is, of course, no longer necessary to use skimmed milk as fixatives are available.

Pastel can be combined with watercolor to great effect, and even with oil monotypes. This is an exciting and flexible medium, and extremely well suited to animals, because you have to move quickly when using the technique, so keeping the liveliness in the picture.

PAPER

Pastels are better used on tonal paper, instead of white, because of the broad spectrum in the lighter color range that would be completely lost on white paper. (In the same way, it is better to wash your white canvas with a medium tone before starting an oil painting, because you can never gauge darkness or lightness properly from a white background.)

Although pastels in themselves are expensive, you can use a surprisingly large range of papers for drawing with pastels, from inexpensive sugar paper to extremely expensive handmade paper. However, the finer the surface, the less pastel you use and the less pastel drops to the bottom of your easel, although some people, after practice, do prefer heavily textured paper or even sandpaper.

RIGHT Pastels can be used very simply and with striking results. Here, just one color manages to convey not just the color of the fur, but also its texture and how light falls on it.

GINGER CAT
BLACK AND WHITE MONOTYPE
WITH PASTEL ON TOP

This cat uses very few pastel colors, and even then they are used sparingly.
Pastels are great for the effective portrayal of thick, fluffy fur.

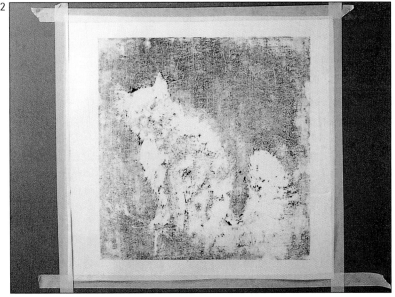

1 I started with the same setup as for a black and white monotype on page 102. You can work from reference or memory.

2 After pulling the black and white print off I strapped it to the board and left it to dry thoroughly.

3 I chose a limited number of pastels as this was not to be a full-blown pastel picture, but a colored drawing. I started with the main color and began to describe the animal's shape and texture. The outline of the coat is important.

4 I used my finger for smudging where necessary—for instance, where the hair is smooth and short over the forehead.

5 I kept the whole picture going, not working on one part for too long. I kept the colors clean and drew with them, rather than laying the pastel down like paint. It was important to step back frequently and see the picture as a whole.

6 I used a good soft white pastel for the white hair around the head and chest, and for defining the head and features; that is where most detail and character will be.

7 I began to draw in the features with soft compressed black charcoal. I tried to put depth into the picture, using the charcoal to bring the cat away from the background.

8 I made sure that I understood the shape the body made under the fluffy coat and tried to show this in my drawing—being careful not to overdo it.

9 If this picture had not succeeded I had my "ghost" print to have a second chance on. I could have turned it into a completely different cat.

OIL PASTELS

Oil pastels are a completely different matter and do not have the luminosity of color enjoyed by chalk pastels. They do not hold the light. They are wonderful for flat areas, creating patterns and excitement but, on the whole, are a rather sticky, heavy medium and not good for delicate subjects such as details of animals or hair texture. One way to use oil pastels is in conjunction with other media. Take turpentine and a brush and use them as you would watercolor, stroking the color onto the paper first, then applying turpentine to produce a wash.

SOFT PASTELS

Once you have found your courage, after practicing with the harder, cheaper end of the market and have an understanding of how to cope with the medium of pastel, you should go on to widening your range of color and softness. It is a good idea to buy a large empty pastel box or have one made with dividers to keep the pastels in line. Or use old cigar boxes; these are good and firm as they are made in wood, but shallow enough to hold the pastels firm so they do not fall about and break.

Soft pastels are a very messy medium and a lot of pastel flakes off and remains in the bottom of the box. One of the best ways of keeping pastels clean is a thin layer of rice over the bottom of the box. This absorbs the excess powder and the roughness of the rice keeps the actual pastels cleaner and gives a soft but firm base on which they can lie. It is a good idea to buy or get the box made much bigger than will hold the number of pastels you actually start with. Range your colors separately; that is, all the reds together, blues, greens etc. by themselves. There are two reasons for this. First, two different color pastels rubbing up against each other, mark each other and make a messy pastel. Second, if you have a space between pastels you will be able to gradually increase your range of colors and shades. I have four boxes each 3 x 2½ feet. with two layers in each. This range has been built up over a considerable number of years for I now know the colors I use most and those I like.

When coming to the end of a color, make sure you do not throw the small piece away, but keep it with others in a separate box and mark it "ends" so you can recognize it with ease. When you go to buy art materials next you will know which ones you have run out of. The softer the pastel, the more brilliant the color and the more you have to look after it. They are a joy to use but you do have to be careful with them. Paying for an expensive pastel, then dropping it and finding most of it as powder on the floor can be very dispiriting.

From the start, even with your cheaper pastels, you should keep them in a safe place, on a steady base and do not move them around too much. Mine are on rollers so that the boxes are not continually picked up and put down. Make sure you put them where your cat cannot jump on them and upset them.

It is also wise to use large flat thumbtacks if using good quality pastel paper because an up and down stroking movement can pull the paper down on the drawing board and tear the paper. Choose an environmentally safe fixative and even so only use it by an open window or preferably in the garden, never near babies, young children or animals. My animals hate it.

ABOVE Soft pastels (top) and hard pastels can both be erased with a normal or putty rubber.

PASTEL DOG AND KITTEN ON TINTED PAPER

I looked at references—photos, sketches, and the animals in real life—and made up my mind exactly what I wanted to see on the paper. I did not hurry to actually put pencil to paper, but took time to look and think, then drew when I was ready.

1 I roughed the picture out rather lightly, getting the main lines down, going from one part to another again and again, relating each part to another. Drawing imaginary lines with your eyes or putting a ruler across the reference to see what parts are in line with each other is useful. I checked the proportions and got the "bones" of the animals in. Remembering that they are solid shapes in space, I placed them within a background, middle, and foreground.

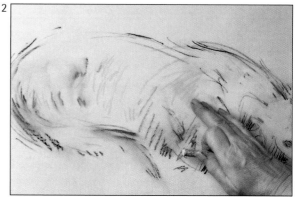

2 I began to bring in color and texture.

3 White chalk was used not only for the color of the coat but to highlight and describe form. By now I had built up the whole body, still constantly checking with my imaginary plumb line and ruler that things were right. I now started to look at detail. The expression and character in the eyes are most important. I used a black pastel on the coat for coloring, but a sharpened black Conté crayon to "draw" with.

4 When drawing two animals like this, make sure they are relating well to each other and that they are both drawn up to the same stage. Now the pastel drawing was well under way. I kept standing back to look. Making a cup of tea or having a sip of wine, depending on the time, I went out of the room for a few minutes and came back to look at the drawing with fresh eyes.

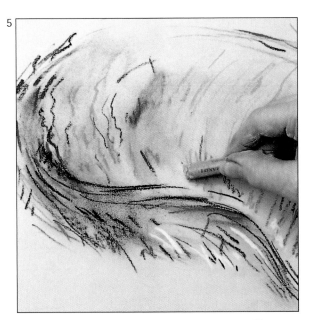

5 Now was the time to adjust any minor mistakes, making sure that the shape of the dog could be seen under his coat.

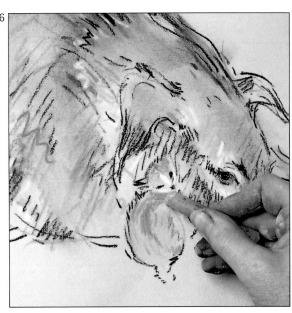

6 In a drawing like this make sure you describe the type of animals portrayed. Here I kept the animals in my mind all the time to convey the characters of my old, kind collie Clarence and a tiny fluffy Manx kitten called Mr. Bill, who became inseparable friends. I stood back frequently to consider the progress of the picture overall.

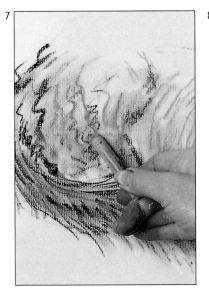

7 I brought up the texture of the coats. This is all important for animals, as would hats, dresses, and textures of materials be if drawing human beings

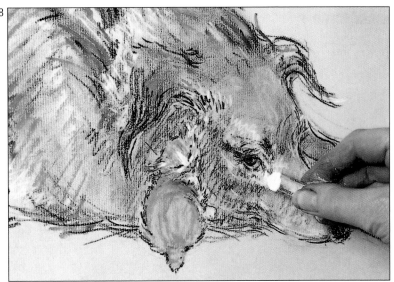

8 A soft white chalk brought the drawing up to its full light potential, the tinted paper giving the middle tones. I used dark orange and black pastels for the dark areas and the white chalk for the lightest ones. Now I had nearly finished I could decide where to strengthen these to give the drawing reality and drama.

9 Some shadow was needed to anchor the animals in the picture and give the dog a base to lie on. Here, it was particularly important because I had not drawn any background.

10 In the finished drawing you can see a good deal of the tinted paper between the pastel strokes; this adds life to the picture.

9
WATERCOLOR

Like pastels, you can also make your own watercolors. The basic ingredients for watercolor are glycerine, distilled water, ox gall, gum arabic, carbolic acid solution, and dry pigment. You need a glass slab, a plastic palette knife, and a glass muller. These ingredients can be bought and you can mix the colors yourself. It is time-consuming, though not difficult. Although this may be exciting to do, it is better for the amateur to buy a good, but limited, box of either watercolor pans or watercolor tubes. Tubes and a palette make mixing colors simpler, but a box is easier to take around with you.

USING WATERCOLOR

When a box of solid watercolors is used, unless you are working very finely and precisely, there is a strong chance of colors running into one another and creating havoc in the box. If you use watercolor tubes, as you would with gouache or oil paints, by squeezing a little at a time onto your palette you keep your paints cleaner and avoid the dangers of disturbing other colors. Tubes for indoor and boxes for outdoor work is probably the best way.

Most subjects can be tackled with a range of 10 or 11 colors, or even bring them down to four—red, green, blue, yellow (and black for line). Again, from a beginner's viewpoint, it is best to start with either these four or a small box. Earth colors, which are the cheapest, are reliable and permanent while "real" ultramarine, for example, is made from pure ground lapis lazuli and costs a fortune. Therefore, until the watercolorist gets a real hold on the techniques it is better to be patient and keep to cheaper materials.

Some watercolors will sink and permeate the paper, while others will remain on the surface layer. The particular attraction of watercolor is its transparency. As this book is about drawing rather than painting I will not discuss painting in watercolor, but just give guidance on wash and line for drawing as well as advising on different types of paper, brushes, and techniques.

ABOVE Watercolor can be used as a wash with pen and ink to create a tighter drawing, or can be used with brush and ink. Watercolor techniques can be used to dramatic effect with paint.

DAPPLE GRAY HORSE
WATERCOLOR AND RAG

As usual, have your references or sketches ready, as this is a spontaneous technique and you do not want to have to look things up when you are in full swing.

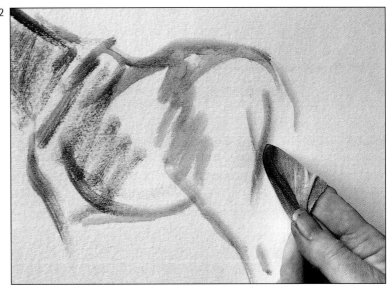

1 I cut a square from a T-shirt small enough to go over my forefinger yet big enough to be held tight by the other fingers. I did not want to drag the cloth over other colors and then across the picture, especially if all was going well. I dipped my cloth-covered finger in the water, rubbed it in the color I wanted and began to draw my subject using my finger just as I would a pencil. The cloth should be as wet as a brush would be, wet enough to move over the paper but not so wet that it drips. I started to draw the main shape remembering my knowledge of the skeleton of this particular animal, placing it so that the whole horse fitted on the paper with room to spare.

2 I checked the perspective and proportions going from the front to the back, noting where the tail was in respect to the shoulders (or withers), where the front legs came under the neck and head and so forth.

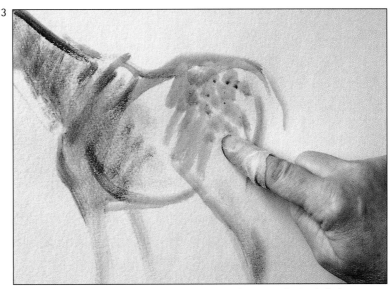

3 Once the drawing was taking shape I started to put in texture. Having built the skeleton, I now put muscle and skin on it.

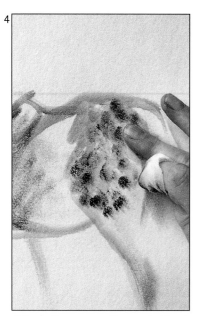

4 I sometimes use my finger only, dipped in paint. Here I dabbed the dapple effect onto the horse's haunches.

5 Keep standing back and reviewing your picture. You will be able to see when you are wrong or overworking areas and mistakes can be put right. I always stand to draw at an easel as it is easier to step back from.

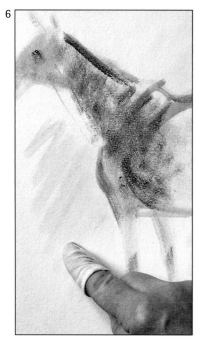

6 I started putting in a little background to give depth and space to the picture.

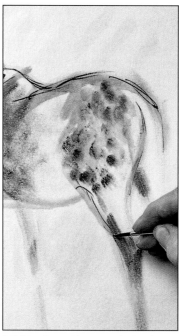

7 With a fine sable watercolor brush, using black paint, I began to draw the details that a finger cannot do—the fine line over the bones, the hock, etc.

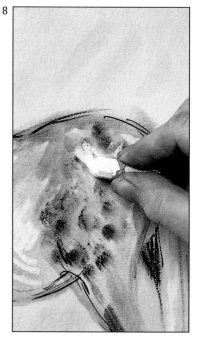

8 I used a very soft white chalk for the texture of dappling and to show the shiny coat of the horse.

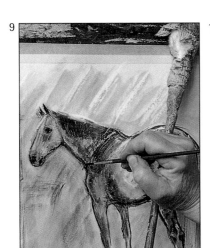

9 Use the brush as you would a pencil or charcoal. Draw freely and with courage or the picture can become fussy and lifeless.

10 Using the fine sable again I added detail with white gouache. Then I put more background in with my finger and a rag. With the brush I defined details such as the head, mane, and hooves.

11 Now that I had nearly finished and could assess how much light I needed in the picture I used chalk again to reinforce highlights.

12 I brought light into the background with broad strokes of the chalk. I added no detail to the background.

13 In the finished picture the light helps to set the horse apart, but also gives the picture depth and atmosphere.

MATERIALS AND EQUIPMENT

Apart from a large and small good solid drawing board there are a number of lightweight collapsible easels to choose from with lightweight folding seats, folding satchels, and compartments in which to keep your equipment if you are drawing outside. You may have a large easel in your studio or workplace if you have sufficient space and motivation, but otherwise the drawing board set against a table and your knees is perfectly adequate for working. I have already outlined this in Chapter 1 (see pages 9–18).

Watercolor and gouache can be used in conjunction with other media and in much broader ways than just with brushes. See the step-by-step demonstration (pages 93–96) which shows painting with a wet rag over your finger dipped in water and color. It is a very free and physically involving way to paint as well as a great deal of fun. A thinner brush with a darker line to paint in the details can then be used. Pieces of dampened cotton wool can be

used to produce the same effect and it is a rather good way of making textures representing fur and hair.

Always remember to have two jars of water; one for washing your brush and one for dipping in paint. If using a box, keep your colors clean. Try to keep your hands and equipment clean and do not panic; if the drawing goes wrong it is not the end of the world. Sometimes if you have overdrawn a watercolor completely, provided you have done it on good-quality paper, it can be hosed down in the shower or scrubbed lightly in cold bathwater. Strap it back down, wait till it is dry and you will be pleasantly surprised

with the effective background you have for further adventures on the same picture.

There are a number of plastic beakers that do not spill when knocked over that are particularly suited to outdoor work, with the good old glass jar for working indoors. It is a good idea to have a range of brushes. The best are sable. Other than that try ox, camel, badger, and squirrel hair brushes. There are also good quality synthetic, cheaper brushes that the beginner may like to start with. It is best to have in your moderate range perhaps a size 000 and go up to a large flat brush for doing washes.

ABOVE AND OPPOSITE Using the dry-brush technique can have the best results when the aim is to specifically capture the roughness or shortness of fur. Bristles and spikes can easily be achieved using this method.

Although you are only drawing in watercolor, using line and wash, it is wise to still use watercolor paper or prepared boards. You can chance it on other sorts of paper but do use wash sparingly if you do. Paper is known as the artist's support as it supports their drawings or paintings. Preferences on weights and texture are only really found out by experiment and practice and the amateur should not start with anything too expensive, such as handmade paper. All papers have a right side; one is smooth, intended for use, and the other slightly rough.

Hot Pressed paper has a hard smooth surface good for pen and ink or line and wash. Cold Pressed paper is a semi-rough paper ideal for big loose washes, but it can also take fine brushwork. The latter is better suited for beginners. There is also very rough paper, which is difficult to control, and rice papers.

When doing line and wash, you should stretch your paper by laying it on the drawing board and strapping it down with masking tape; I cannot emphasize this enough. If you are doing a watercolour painting you may need to damp your paper once you have taped it down with masking tape, but you should not need to if you are drawing with wash.

When laying down large areas of wash it is better to make a large quantity of the color you want to use in your palette so that you do not run out and have to begin again when half the work is already dry. You will also need to paint graduated washes on top of each other to produce a different effect.

The problem with watercolor washes is that they dry extremely quickly. If you want to work into them by laying other washes on top, then glycerine, starch, and salt can be added to the paint to retard this drying process, but it is quite a difficult technique for beginners to cope with.

White gouache ("body color"), on its own, or used in conjunction with watercolor is good for detail. This medium is different from watercolor as it is extended with white pigment, which makes the paint opaque, thus giving the paint more substance or body. When used completely on its own, it produces a much heavier, dense surface; you have to draw on it with a much heavier blacker line, giving a bolder look to your picture, unlike the transparent quality of watercolor, which allows lighter and finer drawing to be used. Body color can be used like white chalk on a tinted background, and is good for highlighting detail as you can see in the Dürer hare drawing.

ABOVE An example of fine detail over layers of dark and light wash with touches of white gouache done by Albrecht Dürer. It is an example not only of fantastic drawing, but also an acute understanding of anatomy together with a fine feeling for this nervous and gentle animal. There is exhaustive detail in the drawing of the hare's coat that does not detract in any way from the overall beauty and excitement of the drawing. This is an exemplary brush and wash picture. Detail sometimes distracts, but in this case only serves to enhance the drawing.

10

MONOTYPES AND DRAWING

Although monotypes are a type of painting, they are included in this book to encourage the amateur to loosen up and enjoy producing pictures. The monotype, or "the painterly print," as it is called, is a combination of painting, drawing, and printing, and a truly exciting way to achieve a picture. Great artists have used this technique from Rembrandt, Lautrec, Lepic, and Degas to the present day.

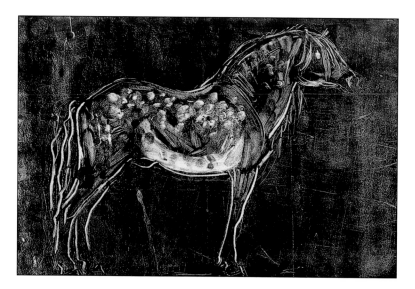

ABOVE **This simple monotype of a horse demonstrates Lepic's technique; a simple line drawing in ink rolled onto a plate which is then printed off onto paper.**

An Italian artist named Giuseppe Castiglione (1610–1668) made the first real monotype, drawing into ink spread on a smooth copper plate around the mid-1640s, while independently in Amsterdam, Rembrandt Van Rijn (1606–1669) was experimenting along similar lines. He began by leaving ink on the surface of the etched plate to create tone and atmosphere, but as far as we know Rembrandt never made a "pure" monotype as Castiglione did.

Between 1660, the date of Castiglione's last monotype and the mid 1870s when Lepic and Degas found the same medium no artist of major importance except for William Blake (1757–1827) used this way of making pictures. Blake painted on milkboard (he had an aversion to oils), so he used tempera.

MAKING A MONOTYPE

The monotype is a technique that has been found and lost again in history, but every artist or student of art who has painted with oils knows a time when they have overworked a painting and it has

become too sticky and wet to go on with. What do you do? You take a sheet of paper, lay it gently but firmly over your soggy painting and lightly pressing down on the painting, smooth over the whole surface with your hand, and taking care not to smudge the painting, pull the paper off. Voila! You have a monotype. You then strap this to a board and begin work on it if you wish when it is dry. This pulling off brings with it the essential darks, lights, and color of the painting without the detail, making it feel fresh and immediate against the overworked picture it had become.

Rembrandt's and Castiglione's techniques went further; they had started leaving "plate tone" on etching plates. Lepic began rolling ink onto unetched plates and, wiping or drawing with a tool or his finger into the ink, then printing from this. This achieved one print and a "ghost," a very faint second

print. With etching you can ink up the plate again and again, producing exactly the same print until the plate wears out. Monotypes are different, however, as you only have one print and a ghost. This process led Degas to experiment, and he produced sensual and erotic nudes in black and white. In turn, this led to the use of color and many artists took it up from there including Lautrec, Gauguin, Picasso, and later De Kooning and many others.

There are many different methods of producing a variety of effects, but there are one or two basic techniques. If you have a printing press or an old mangle, you can use pieces of thin flat steel (you can buy these from builders' suppliers, lumberyards, and chandlers). The mangle or press will produce the pressure to print your picture onto paper. If not, you can use heavy books or weights for pressure. In this case you can use not only steel to paint and draw your picture on, but any nonporous surface such as formica, or even glass, but do be very careful when using glass as it can break under too much pressure.

Compressed charcoal is best for drawing onto prints when they are dry, or you can use a French blue oil pastel to good effect as well. Limit your palette as monotypes can be messy, especially for beginners. Oil sticks and oil pastels can also be used. Gauguin used watercolors but it is thought he printed off from cardboard (which is a very difficult technique). I have made gouache and watercolor monotypes on steel; gouache gives a better effect than watercolor, but you have to work quickly as it dries so fast. Oil or printing ink is best for beginners.

GAZELLE
BLACK AND WHITE MONOTYPE

This is the simple and basic procedure for producing a black and white monotype.

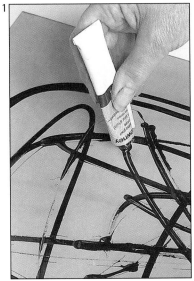

1 I put some newspaper on the table and placed the plate on top. I squeezed enough black printing ink onto the plate in strips across it.

2 I smoothed the ink with the rubber printing roller across the plate, backward and forward and up and down until I achieved an even black surface.

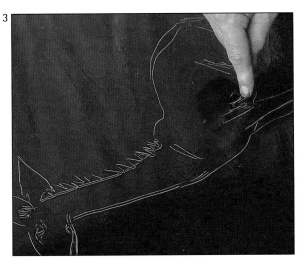

3 With my fingernail (sometimes I use the end of a brush) I boldly drew in the lines of the picture, making sure I scraped through the ink to the plate.

4 Using a piece of smooth cotton material (here a piece of old T-shirt cut into three or four squares) wetted with turpentine till damp, not dripping, I pulled the ink off the plate where texture or shading was needed.

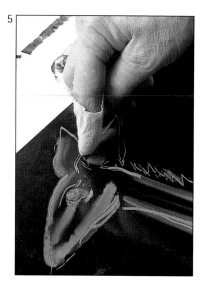

5 Pulling the cloth tightly over my forefinger I drew the shape with it where I thought the line needed strengthening.

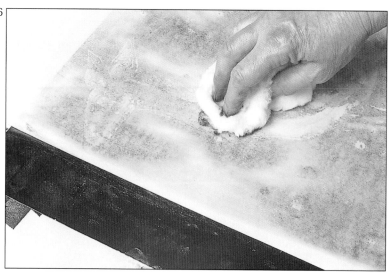

6 Cutting the paper slightly larger than the plate, I laid it gently down over the plate, being careful not to move or smudge it.

Holding it down with one hand, with a piece of cloth soaked in turpentine I gently wiped over the paper, without soaking it (some people find it easier to wet the paper beforehand and keep it somewhere clean).

I put an extra piece of clean cartridge paper over the top, then placed heavy books on top of that and left it for a while. If you are lucky enough to have a press or old mangle put it through the press between blankets.

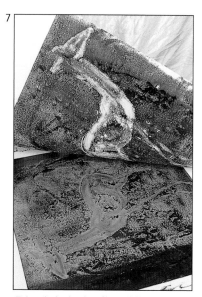

7 I took the books off carefully and removed the top piece of paper. I gently pulled the print away from the plate by the corner, then immediately strapped it down with masking tape on a clean piece of hardboard and left it to dry completely.

ABOVE **Monotype of a goat. The technique is suited to many animals.**

CART HORSE
COLORED MONOTYPE

Employing the same methods with different media can produce a vast range
of fun results. Compare this horse with the black and white cat used
on pages 84–86.

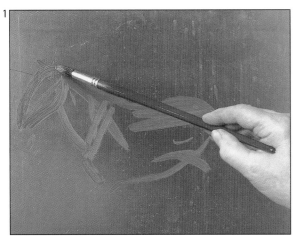

1 I chose the subject and colors, having everything ready as I did not want the paints to start drying off. My subject here is a chestnut cart horse. I made sure the drawing was bold, setting out the main shapes. If you go wrong with this technique you can just wipe off the ink with a wet rag damped in turpentine.

2 I placed good strong color onto the plate.

3 I worked more color in using bold strokes.

4 Details were painted in with a finer brush, using a good amount of paint. If you are too detailed at this point, nothing will come out in the print.

5 Texture was stippled in with a broader brush.

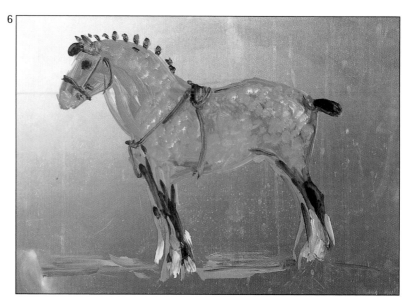

6 Now the picture was ready to print.

7 Continuing exactly as for a black and white monotype, I put my dampened paper gently down over the plate. I placed blank covering paper over and put weights on top. (If you have a press or mangle then you can put the plate through and print.) After leaving it for a while I took off the weights and cover paper.

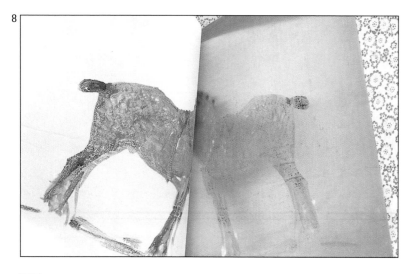

8 The print was lifted off, then strapped down to a board and left to dry.

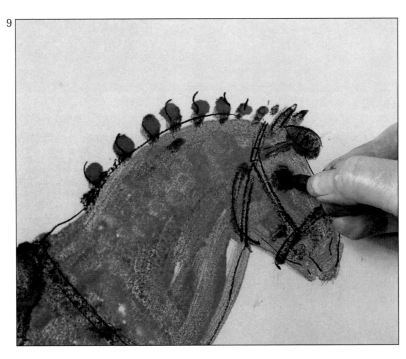

9 With a piece of soft compressed charcoal I drew in details.

10 The finished picture was bold, its strong lines emphasizing the character of the cart horse.

PAPER

Any paper will do, but white throws the color up brilliantly and gives you more scope when drawing on top once the print is dry. If you use colored paper, as you would with pastels, work with lighter chalks and use good strong cartridge paper, or even board, as it takes the turpentine and paint without buckling.

With color, you are painting a picture and printing it, the drawing on top making the line, rather than scraping away the pigment to make the lines as with black and white. You are preparing a "ground" on which you can draw later either with a blue or black line, or with pastels, or using both as Degas did.

Always remember that everything you do will be reversed. So when you come to draw over a print, you will be seeing it in reverse. You can hold the original up to the mirror to see it in its original form, but this is difficult and time consuming, and takes away the spontaneity.

Once you get your courage up, making monotypes is great fun.

When my daughter was young, many an afternoon was spent in the yard with groups of tiny children, painting with big brushes, on pieces of formica and producing dozens of exciting monotypes, to the amazement and delight of their mothers, to take home.

BELOW For my poster of *Flamingos by Tube* I used glass to paint on, and books to press the cartridge paper down to print. They were difficult to work with, because of their large size and I had to use lots of books and a blower heater to dry them with.

HORSE AND DOG IN CIRCUS RING
COLORED MONOTYPE ON TINTED PAPER

This technique can be used to create more abstract images. You can never be quite sure how they will come out, and this makes them exciting.

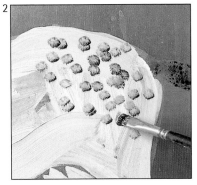

1 My subject came from my imagination— a horse and dog in a circus ring. I painted boldly, using more light colors than usual, and applying them thickly. This would show up when I finally printed on the tinted paper. You can use more dark or more light oil colors to determine how light or dark the picture should be.

2 After putting in the main shape, I started working on the texture. The horse is a dapple gray, so I put in the markings on his coat.

3 A stipple brush was used to good effect.

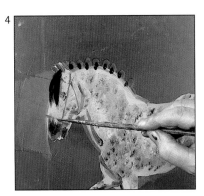

4 For smaller places or detail I used a finer brush.

5 This is not a painting, but I put in background to place the horse and dog in the circus. I drew the circus tent and ring using a bold line.

6 You can see that I put in whiter strips to produce light. I also painted the dog in.

7 I printed the plate as for a black and white monotype, but instead of using white cartridge paper I used tinted pastel paper. I chose a mid cream color because I wanted a halfway tone to bring up the lights and darks in the picture. This paper is lighter in weight than cartridge, so more care was taken when dampening it with turpentine before laying it on the plate, and when putting it down on the plate.

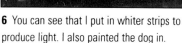

8 The paint in the pulled-off print "swam" a little; this is usual in colored monotypes. The colors move and merge together. If this happens do not worry about it; just use any new developments that may take place to add life to the picture. I strapped the picture down and left it to dry.

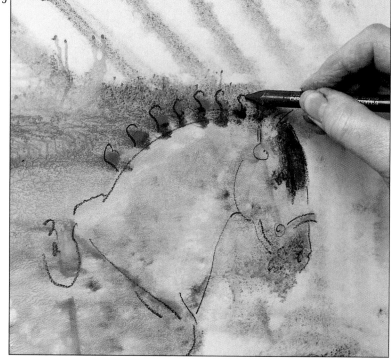

9 Once dry the picture was ready for more work. I used a darkish French blue crayon to draw with. Sometimes a blue line is more subtle than black and gives a different look to the picture. I made the red details on the harness stand out by drawing a blue line round them. This use of the line is the essential difference between drawing and painting.

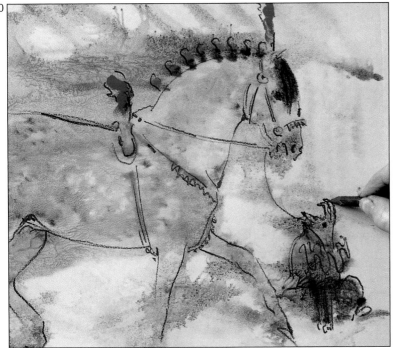

10 I put in the details of the dog, then added details to the horse's head.

11 The finished drawing has a lively feel to it. Sometimes, if you are drawing from imagination, you may like to do a rough first, so that when you add the details you already know what you want.

11

SKETCHBOOKS

A sketchbook is a notebook. It is not for finished drawings, rather it is for catching the fleeting moment, a small detail, something important you may wish to refer to and use later on. It should be the artist's constant companion and as private as a personal diary. In the pages of the sketchbook you should include quick studies of real life, snatches of interesting things seen, workouts for composition, for ideas for future pictures that you may have when sitting on a train, a bus, or in a restaurant. If not put down directly the moment will vanish.

Just as authors keep pads by them for notes, so the artist should use a sketchbook, not just for ideas from real life but for pictures from the imagination. I have kept a sketchbook of my dreams for many years. Look at Chagall's and Frida Kahlo's pictures based on dreams. Used in this way a sketchbook can lead you up many byways, to many areas such as symbolism, or even abstraction. Sketchbooks are a kind of graphic memory.

USING A SKETCHBOOK

It is better to use something easily carried, that does not smudge. There are many good fiber-tipped pens available of varying sizes and texture of point and you can use a combination of materials. Felt-tip

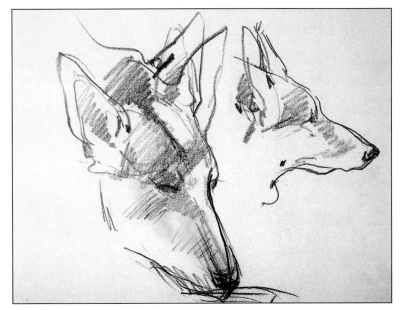

ABOVE Use sketches to practice drawing just one feature of a subject from different angles. It is important to be able to show perspective accurately in all positions.

BELOW A standing elephant. There is particular stress on conveying the perspective of the animal from behind, and getting the foreshortening right, without it looking awkward.

ABOVE Foreshortening is incredibly important when an animal is sitting, or lying down. There will always be a part of the body, that is there, but is invisible to the eye. You must be able to describe this in your drawing.

BELOW It can take very few strokes of a pencil to capture the line of an animal, its shape and form.

pens are great for color as you can use them quite broadly and they will not buckle the paper. They can be drawn over with black fiber-tipped pen, Conté or ink. But make sure your felt-tip top is on tightly as the tips dry out quickly.

You can never have too many sketchbooks. Some working artists have piles of them and often keep them categorized on a year-by-year basis or based on subject, so that the work can be referred to at any time by its title or year. For a beginner, I suggest three sketchbooks would be enough, one of them a small one that should be kept always in the pocket, handbag,

or briefcase, with a couple of good, reliable fiber-tipped pens. This will give you easy access to quick drawing wherever you are. This small sketchbook should be hard-backed as it needs to be hardwearing for travel.

A middle-sized spiral-bound sketchbook may be carried if you are going on a trip to the zoo, or out to the country where you need a hard back or support to the paper but do not want to drag around a drawing board. By being bigger, it can accommodate a more important style of drawing, more information, and more color. The spiral binding will enable you to

ABOVE Preliminary sketches of a ram. In each one the all-knowing, ever-watchful eye of the animal has become the one dominant feature.

BELOW Sketches do not have to define just the line of an animal and its position, but can also capture the nature of its fur, skin, and coloring.

ABOVE Rough sketches of a rhinoceros. There is a very definite description of the thick heavy folds of skin, without any texture having actually been put on. Capturing this is important should you wish to use a sketch as reference for a drawing.

RIGHT This elephant is definitely on the move. There is a skill in capturing the power and purpose in his stride, an understanding of its character and anatomy.

pull the pictures out and use them as reference if you wish.

The third is a big, spiral-bound, drawing book that you should keep at home or, if going on a trip, keep in your drawing satchel. This still gives you the facility of paper on a hard back without a drawing board, which, unlike block paper, enables you to turn over the page. This big sketchbook can be used for whole pictures as well as parts of pictures. Whole compositions and subjects can be done in it. If, by chance, you do a good finished drawing, it can be easily extracted from the sketchbook.

If you are going to do a picture at say, the zoo, or a farm, and you

have done lots of sketches of either background movement or detail for another picture, it is useful to pull the drawings out of the sketchbook and stick them with masking tape around the wall so that instead of having to constantly turn the pages of your book, all your references for that particular picture are in front of you, to help and inspire you. There is nothing like sticking a drawing on the wall and looking at it over a period of time to find out how good or bad it is. Of course, large sketchbooks can be used in classes but I suggest paper on drawing board for this as it allows you to use any technique and you cannot put a drawing pad up on an easel.

ABOVE **The inspiration behind the drawing of the gazelles on page 67. Note the graceful nature of the creatures, which could easily have been lost if drawing from a photograph.**

12

EXPANDING YOUR SKILLS— MAKING A MAQUETTE

Just as singers or pianists have to practice their scales, so artists have to practice their drawing. No one wants to listen to a singer pushing his voice to extremes, trying out techniques and doing breathing exercises or a pianist doing scales. So you should keep your practice drawings to yourself, as most people will not understand them.

Sketches, when they are undertaken as sketches, especially of moving animals, are very different from finished drawings; "working drawings," in turn, are different from both of them. They are not finished work, ready to be framed.

WORKING DRAWINGS

Many beginners are under the impression that everything they do should be good enough to show others or, equally, so bad they must be thrown away. As a student at the Royal Academy in 1956, I was, on one occasion, particularly satisfied with a nude I had been "shining up." My teacher, Mr Fleetwood Walker RA, stood behind me, and tucking his fingers into his waistcoat pockets he murmured, "I wouldn't sign that if I were you," and moved on to the next student. No more needed to be said—the drawing was quickly thrown in the wastebasket.

You have to find a middle way when learning—to have enough confidence to try to have a go, to take criticism and to experience joy and excitement in what you are doing without expecting to become an accomplished artist overnight and "sign your drawings" as I so nearly did. Yet, on the other hand, you must learn not to hide your work or be so woefully shy that you let no one see it, and, therefore, never progress.

Drawing before doing a piece of sculpture, is quite different from drawing for a painting in life school. In the sculpture class you can make a huge mess of the drawing in the end in an effort to explain to yourself (*not* to others) where the weight is, how the shoulders and hips drop; and at what angles the head and arms are, how big or small the figure is and the whole "line" of what you are about to try to describe in clay. This drawing will be a mess but it will be a success as a working sculptural drawing and you will have learnt so very much from doing it.

Start with the armature in your drawing as you would a skeleton, then "hang" the body on to that. If the armature is wrong in a structure it will always fall down. So force yourself to draw in this way, freeing yourself from just making pretty marks on paper. Instead, you will be using methods that will make you understand, which will help you later on to draw well, not showing the black charcoal scrubbed on, or the circles drawn round and round the limbs, or the line of the armature. Finally you will have learnt your scales and will be able to sing an aria.

BELOW Anything can be used as a reference from which to base a maquette; a sketch, a photograph, a finished drawing, or, as here, a monotype. The image is striking and one that will work well as a three-dimensional study.

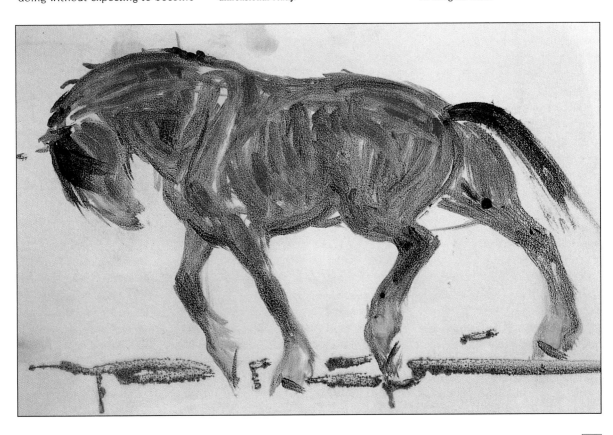

PULLING CART HORSE
SCULPTURAL DRAWING AND MAQUETTE

The monotype on the previous page proved an inspiration for developing into a maquette.

Materials for Maquette

Piece of wood or firm base.
Wire of two weights: one thin enough to bend, but fat enough to stand up, and some electrical or other thin, very flexible wire.
Nails: U-shaped nails are best.
A pack of modeling clay. If you have a few modeling tools, use them, but for such a rough maquette fingers are fine, and you can feel the shape you are making. This is, of course, a learning exercise, as well as a basic sculpture lesson.

1

1 I chose a cart horse pulling something heavy for my subject, because the large shape of the horse, the strong neck, and the heavy muscular rump, show very plainly the strong line this horse makes when doing this action.

I first looked at my subject for some time, and thought of what the skeleton would look like. I asked myself which legs the weight would be on and, because of which legs would be bearing the weight, how did this slant the hip bones and push the head forward and down. This horse is heavy and is pulling a heavy load. Every line in the drawing and sculpture should tell the viewer this.

If you are drawing from reference, you could place a piece of tracing paper over the subject and "draw" the main lines as suggested on pages 54–55. With moving animals, if you are drawing from life or following sketches from life, then the same main lines should be made over the top. Do not worry about "pretty" drawing; this is drawing for a particular reason.

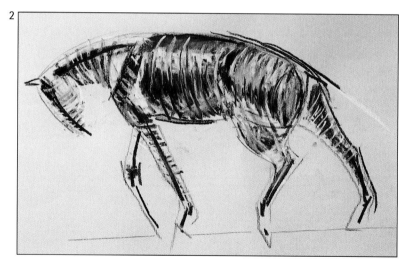

2

2 Next, I looked at the main shapes of the horse, the round ribs, the heavily muscled neck, and rump, trying to imagine the animal and what these massive muscles would feel like if I stroked him. Also, how they would change from him standing still to lunging forward and putting his weight against the collar (I did not put the harness in—the head goes down, the front legs, chest, and withers take the strain, and the back legs push and hold.

I drew round and round first with black charcoal. Then, with white chalk making a very solid shape, I drew over this again. You could even use another color if you liked to help explain and accentuate the shape and strength of this animal and the line he makes as he pulls. It is useful to do as many of these initial drawings explaining this to yourself as you like.

3

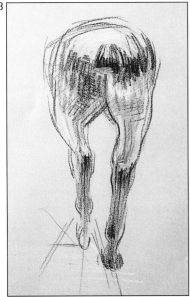

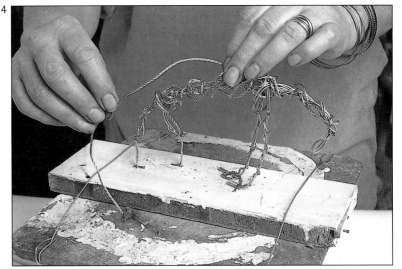

3 I drew the horse from every angle. Note how the hindquarters slope if one hind leg is dropped lower than the other back supporting leg. Note also how the haunches are lower with the effort of pulling and that the withers (shoulders) are then the highest point. I chose a horse, but the same principles would apply to any animal—a dog pointing, a cat stretching, an elephant shifting its weight. It is really important to try to understand what a particular animal is doing and what happens to its body in the process.

4 I now turned my attention to the maquette. I made sure the piece of wood was big enough to support the little sculpture and thick enough for the nails. The wood should be strapped onto something solid; I strapped mine on a turntable, but a heavier piece of wood would do.

I then looked at my drawing, and made a shape with the heavy wire directly like the main lines in the drawing. I bent the wire for the feet and nailed these to the wood, pushing the wire to make the right skeleton. When the legs were held down firmly, I used the lighter wire to wind round and round the thicker one. I did not

do this tightly since it is there to make the rough shapes and hold the clay on. It is only necessary to wind it tightly when you need to hold things together such as where the legs and body meet at the hip and shoulders.

I made sure everything was balanced and strong enough to hold the clay. If you are making something with thick shapes, an animal lying down or an elephant, for instance, the wire can be supported by using matchsticks held tightly by the wire, or bound on with masking or other tape. If the body is large, newspaper stuffed inside helps to build the sculpture up and fill the space.

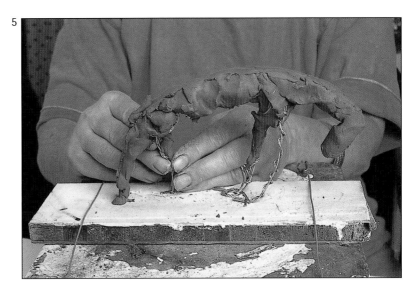

5 I started putting the clay on, pressing it between the wire, working on the main shape.

6 I kept the whole sculpture going at once, turning it round to see it from every angle, constantly checking with my drawing. The more thorough the drawing, the more knowledge there is to help with the sculpture.

7 I did not go into great detail. If, looking at a maquette, the viewer gets the same feeling as when looking at the original photo or references then it has succeeded. Do not worry if the first attempt is not exactly right. Next time it will be better, and every time the artist learns something as well as having fun.

13

PRESENTATION AND CARE OF WORK

Make a rigid rule that you do not interrupt your flow of creativity by wiping tables and clearing things away and tidying up. There is plenty of time for that when you have exhausted your strength on more important areas; but no matter how tired you are at the end of the day, if you get into the routine, you can do your tidying up in an almost zombie-like fashion.

Brushes *must* be cleaned and stacked, heads up, in jars that do not overturn easily. Excess paint must be cleaned from your palettes; drawings not wanted thrown away. The floor must be swept and the place generally made ready for the next day.

TAKING CARE OF YOUR WORK

Especially in drawing animals, you need clean sketchbooks, sharpened pencils, and Contés in labeled boxes, in places you can easily reach at any moment. A certain light on a cat curled up in a chair by an open window can be completely lost while you are running around looking for drawing materials. Always make sure you have a good stock of non-acid tissue paper to put in between drawings to save them from smudging if you are working with soft pastels or chalk.

Try to have a large flat drawer—a plan chest is ideal—in which to keep your charcoal and pastel drawings with acid-free tissue between them. If you slide charcoal or pastel into a folder, the act of dropping or sliding down and past other drawings will damage them. They must be kept flat. If possible, when handling your drawings, keep your hands and your surfaces dry and clean.

Make sure you have a small stock of glass jars, cigar boxes, and large plastic containers with their tops cut off. Any solution in which you are going to put your brushes should be labeled. Only buy the items you need. Do not waste your shelf space with a lot of equipment that will cost you a great deal of money and that you will never use. All paper that is not in books or blocks should be kept flat. There is nothing worse than pinning up a deliciously tinted piece of pastel paper or a big piece of cartridge ready to draw then finding it has become corrugated because it has been stood on end and buckled under its own weight.

If you are using an easel and pastels, it is a good idea to use a dustpan and brush, then a damp cloth to clean the pastel from the shelf of the easel on which your drawing board rested. This needs to be done after every day's work and you will be surprised how much dust you find there. The softer the pastel, the more dust you will find. Try not to breathe it in, or wear a mask, and do not let children or babies breathe it in.

Always have a bag full of soft rags tied to your easel as well as two or three different widths of masking tape hung on a rope tied to your easel. It is useful to always have these at hand. The rags can be used for dusting off charcoal, used on your fingers as a painting technique, or for mopping up spilt turpentine or glasses of wine. If you do not have studio space it is good to have something to put on the floor to protect it so that you do not walk pastel dust over the rest of the house.

MOUNTING AND FRAMING

If you reach the stage where you think you can handle mounting and framing, there are many books on this subject. If someone decides they will buy or commission a work, and wish to pay you for it, either decide on your price and get the framing done for them and charge for the framing as well, or just charge for the picture and set up a friendly relationship with a good and reliable framer to whom you can recommend your clients.

Mounting and framing is, in itself, an art. If you are lucky enough to get past the interim stage of being an artist who does their own framing and become too busy to do it yourself, you will be a lucky and happy person if you find a framer. A good framer understands how to enhance an artist's work. Indeed, a framer can make or break a drawing or painting. Never underestimate the framer's skills.

BELOW AND OPPOSITE **These charcoal drawings of zebras and giraffes were both done in one sitting at a zoo. They are in simple cardboard mounts, which confines and defines the space they occupy. Stephen Crowther.**

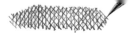

CUTTING A MOUNT FOR YOUR WORK

If you want to present your work properly, it is important to learn how to cut a mount. Easy to master, it is a skill that will benefit your work tremendously.

1

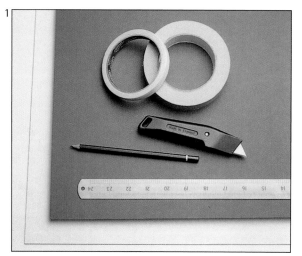

1 These are the basic tools you will need. The mountboard, craft knife, steel ruler, masking and double-sided tape.

2

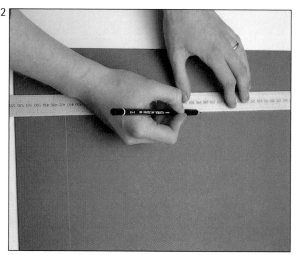

2 Measure and draw the lines for the window mount.

3

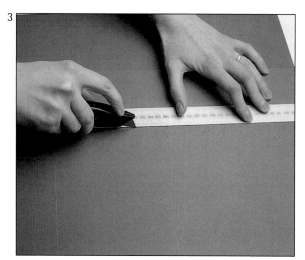

3 Cut window mount. This type of ruler is adequate but heavier steel rulers with rubber bases are safer.

4

4 Lifting out the cutout from the window board. Save this piece of board; it may serve for a smaller drawing.

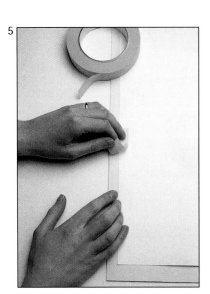

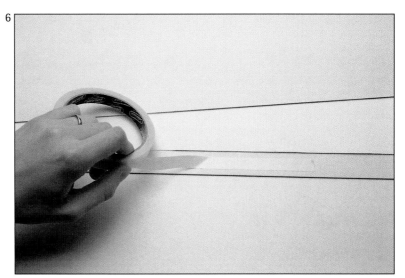

5 Tape the drawing into position on the window mount. If the drawing is a pastel or other delicate, easily-smudged media, it should be laid face-down on tracing paper to keep it from smudging.

6 Stick the back board onto the window mount with double-sided tape.

7 The finished drawing in its mount. Tracing paper can be put over this if it is to be stored away.

INDEX